GOD'S GLORIOUS
CHURCH

GOD'S GLORIOUS CHURCH

The Mystery and Mission of the Body of Christ

Tony Evans

MOODY PUBLISHERS
CHICAGO

All Scripture quotations, unless otherwise indicated, are taken from the *New American Standard Bible*®, © Copyright The Lockman Foundation 1960, 1962, 1963, 1968, 1971, 1972, 1973, 1975, 1977, 1995. Used by permission.

Scripture quotations marked NIV are taken from the *Holy Bible, New International Version*®. NIV®. Copyright © 1973, 1978, 1984 by International Bible Society. Used by permission of Zondervan Publishing House. All rights reserved.

Scripture quotations marked KJV are taken from the King James Version.

ISBN: 0-8024-3951-9

1 3 5 7 9 10 8 6 4 2

Printed in the United States of America

This book is lovingly dedicated to
all the members of
Oak Cliff Bible Fellowship
for the strategic part they play
in helping us to be God's Glorious Church

CONTENTS

PART THREE
THE FUNCTION OF THE CHURCH

GOD'S GLORIOUS
CHURCH

GOD'S GLORIOUS CHURCH

The Mystery and Mission of the Body of Christ

Tony Evans

MOODY PUBLISHERS
CHICAGO

© 2003 by
ANTHONY T. EVANS

ISBN: 0-8024-3951-9

1 3 5 7 9 10 8 6 4 2

Printed in the United States of America

*This book is lovingly dedicated to
all the members of
Oak Cliff Bible Fellowship
for the strategic part they play
in helping us to be God's Glorious Church*

CONTENTS

PART THREE
THE FUNCTION OF THE CHURCH

WITH GRATITUDE

I want to say a word of thanks to my friend and editor, Philip Rawley, for his excellent help in the preparation of this manuscript, and to Greg Thornton, Cheryl Dunlop, and the rest of the team at Moody Publishers for their encouragement and quality work on this project.

INTRODUCTION

This is a book about the local church, the most important spiritual institution in human history. It is the visible manifestation of the universal church (all Christians from Pentecost to the Rapture) in history. That means nothing is more important for us than understanding what God wants us to learn about the church, and participating in a local assembly of believers who are seeking to live out the principles and precepts of the kingdom of God.

Although we are saved individually, as Christians we are born into a community. Just as a baby must be born into the context of a family in order to experience the fullness of his new life, so each of us must become a functioning member of God's new household, the church, in order to experience the fullness of the new life we possess.

This means that local churches must understand their identity and purpose for their existence, and provide a biblically healthy context for believers to grow and live out their lives by faith. It's unfortunate that so many churches see themselves primarily as weekly centers of spiritual inspiration for their parishioners, rather than the only ordained place where heaven visits earth. When we do church right, God's people will experience and reflect the answer to Jesus' prayer, "Your kingdom come. Your will be done, on earth as it is in heaven" (Matthew 6:10).

It is my hope that this book will enable you not only to understand what the church is, but also inspire you to help make your place of worship all that God intends it to be.

THE NATURE OF THE CHURCH

1
THE IMPORTANCE OF THE CHURCH

All of us are familiar with the story of Humpty Dumpty, the figure from the children's nursery rhyme whose world was shattered after he had a great fall. He called on the best his world had to offer to address his problem—"all the king's horses and all the king's men." We would say today that Humpty had the White House, the Congress, the military, and any other human power or authority you can think of coming to his aid in his brokenness.

But the tragedy of the story is that none of these human powers could put Humpty Dumpty's life and world back together again. Apparently Mr. Dumpty had no biblically functioning church available to help him, because if he had he would not have had to call on the king in the first place.

Now it's one thing when a nursery rhyme character cannot find the help he needs to repair his shattered world, even when his problem is being attended to by the highest authorities the culture has to offer. But it's another thing altogether when real people in the real world discover that all the king's horses and all the king's men—human institutions of power and influence—can't fix society's deepest problems and address people's deepest needs.

This is where the church comes in, because the church is the most important institution on earth. The church, and only the church, has been commissioned by the sovereign Lord to be His representative agency in history. It has been given sole authority to unlock the treasures of the spiritual realm so that they can be brought to bear on the realities of earth.

Thus, as the church goes so goes everything else. God designed the church to be the epicenter of culture, and the church's strength or weakness is a major determining factor in the success or failure of human civilization. When the church is strong, the culture is impacted positively—even if the "powers that be" in a particular place don't realize that impact and seek to marginalize and persecute the church. But when the church is weak, its influence deteriorates and so does the culture.

One example of the church's impact, both positively and negatively, is the institution of slavery in America. Many segments of American culture condoned and sanctioned slavery, even though it served as the catalyst for a civil war that cost thousands of lives and helped produce ongoing cultural upheaval. And Christendom at large helped provide justification for slavery, even leading some to find a basis for slavery in Scripture. But, in the end, it was the strength of the true church bringing its influence to bear that helped lead to the collapse of slavery.

It is important to understand the church's importance for cultural reasons, since Jesus called His people to be salt and light, a city on a hill. But understanding the church's nature and mission is even more important for spiritual reasons. That's because the church has been given the assignment of growing all of its members into mature believers who can disciple others and maximize their spiritual potential.

When the church is strong, its members recognize their eternal purpose and the church moves forward. But when the church is weak, its members tend to wander around in confusion on their spiritual pilgrimage. My purpose and prayer for this book is that it will contribute to our understanding of the church, so that instead of being Humpty Dumptys lying in ruins with no one to help us, we will become dynamic followers of Jesus Christ and contributing members of His church.

A GOD-SIZED PROBLEM

Talking about the church may bring certain verses from the Bible to your mind. But I want to begin our discussion of the church in what seems like an unusual place—not in the words of Jesus or the writings of Paul, but in an obscure Old Testament passage in which we find a God-sized problem that will help us answer the question of why the church is so important in God's plan today.

Before we go to this passage, let me give you a foundational principle for this chapter and this book, which is simply this: Everything that is physical and visible—the world and life around us—is controlled by things that are invisible and spiritual. This has always been the case, in fact. We need to get this order straight because the only real way to fix what is wrong in the visible and physical realm is to make sure that the invisible and spiritual realm is working right. Until the invisible is operating properly, the visible cannot be addressed in any lasting and effective way. This is why society can go on for years and even centuries without seeing very basic and destructive problems being solved, no matter how much clout and money we throw at those issues.

A Time of Great Chaos

Keeping this principle in mind, I want to deal with our passage, 2 Chronicles 15:3–6, where the writer looks back to an earlier period in Israel's history. The prophet Azariah was urging King Asa of Judah to continue the reforms he had begun. To reinforce his message, Azariah reminded Asa of the sad condition God's people were in during an earlier age, which many Bible commentators believe was the period of the judges. If so, Azariah was speaking of Israel's low point spiritually when he said, "For many days Israel was without the true God and without a teaching priest and without law" (v. 3).

Verse 4 refers to those times when Israel sought God during that period, but in verses 5–6 the prophet summarized those days of chaos and God's judgment: "In those times there was no peace to him who went out or to him who came in, for many disturbances afflicted all the inhabitants of the lands. Nation was crushed by nation, and city by city, for God troubled them with every kind of distress."

Several things from these verses are worth noting. For instance, the description of a society in the grip of violence, crime, and conflict between nations sounds like our world today, so we know there's a lesson for us here. Like the world of ancient Israel, our culture is also in chaos and confusion.

But what ought to grab your attention is the statement in verse 6 that this all came about because "God troubled" the people. We might have expected Azariah to say that this mess was the result of satanic activity and influence in the world. According to the prophet, however, God was the author of this confusion among the people, although He was not in any way the author of their sin that provoked His judgment.

In other words, these problems that were tearing apart the fabric of society had a spiritual cause. So to address the lack of peace on a social level, try to deal with violence and crime through more law enforcement, or settle conflicts between governments at the bargaining table would not be sufficient because the people's problem was with God. And when God is your problem, God alone is your solution.

What was it about this period of Israel's history that caused God to "trouble" His people with distress at so many levels? The root of the problem is found in 2 Chronicles 15:3. Three key elements that are necessary to keep God's people on track spiritually were missing.

A Lack of True Knowledge

The first of these elements was the lack of "the true God." This does not say that God had withdrawn Himself from Israel so that the people forgot who He was or could no longer find Him. Even in the days of the judges, there was religious service going on in Israel. People were offering sacrifices to God. But it was not the kind of authentic religion that pleased God or produced the right kind of response from Him.

We could say that the Israelites had forgotten the kind of holy God they were serving, so they thought nothing of going off into idolatry or mixing with pagans or violating His law in a dozen other ways. Israel was living as if it couldn't tell the one true God from the many false gods around it. Spiritual activity was going on, but it wasn't true to God's requirements.

A Lack of Biblical Teaching

What could have caused God's people to get all confused about the nature of God and start mixing the true with the false? In the case before us, the second phrase of 2 Chronicles 15:3 gives us a large clue. In those days, "Israel was . . . without a teaching priest." We would say today that the nation had a very serious pastoral problem —a mist in the pulpit that became a fog in the pew, as we'll see later.

Notice that the text does not say that Israel had no priests. The problem was that the priests were not carrying out their function of teaching God's law so the people would know the true God and what He expected of them. The priests were doing an inadequate job of providing a divine viewpoint through which the people could interpret all of life and make God-honoring decisions.

Now don't misunderstand. People are responsible for their own relationship to God and their obedience to His revealed will, especially in a day like today when we each have a copy of God's Word and the ability to read it. But I'm talking about a systemic spiritual failure at the heart of Israel's spiritual leadership that kept the people uninformed and ill-informed about their responsibility before God and the consequences of failing to meet it.

A Lack of Correct Application

The third problem mentioned in 2 Chronicles 15:3 follows as a natural consequence of the first two. Because the people didn't know their God intimately and were not hearing His Word taught, they were "without law." That is, they didn't know how to apply God's law to the situations they faced. The divine rules weren't being applied, so people made up their own.

The last phrase of the last verse of the book of Judges illustrates this problem perfectly: "Everyone did what was right in his own eyes" (Judges 21:25). Everybody had an idea of what to do, but nothing worked because God's government of His people was not being upheld and enforced.

We hear a lot today about the separation of church and state. They ought to be separate because they are two distinct institutions with two distinct jurisdictions. But what cannot be separated is God and His role in society, because people will always live by some governing principle, whether good or bad.

The people of Israel didn't know how to bring God's truth to bear on their world, and the practical result was that they lived as if no divine framework existed at all.

Look at our nation today. How can we have all of these churches on every corner with all of these preachers and programs and facilities, and yet still have such moral and spiritual chaos in our culture? It's because we, as God's people, aren't bringing His Word and His power to bear on the world around us, so people are living as if God doesn't exist. But that's another issue, and we'll come back to it later.

A GOD-ORDAINED SOLUTION

Since the basic realities of spiritual conflict and the superior power of the spiritual world haven't changed since the days of the judges in ancient Israel, we see the same principle of the visible world being controlled by the invisible world at work today. Paul gave us one of the clearest statements of this reality in Ephesians 6:12 when he said, "Our struggle is not against flesh and blood, but against the rulers, against the powers, against the world forces of this darkness, against the spiritual forces of wickedness in the heavenly places."

This is also a great statement of why the church is central to God's plan. God has always had a vehicle or an agency on earth to make His presence manifest, carry out His will, and bring what is invisible and spiritual down to the world of the visible and the physical.

Israel's system of the law, the sacrifices, and the priesthood was God's agency to accomplish His program on earth in the Old Testament. Today that agency is the church and only the church. Now that doesn't mean God cannot reveal Himself to someone apart from the visible presence of a church. But the Bible is clear that the church is the entity that brings the realm of heaven into history and brings the values of heaven to bear on earth. To put it another way, the church is the answer to Jesus' prayer, "Your will be done, on earth as it is in heaven" (Matthew 6:10).

Jesus' Promise of the Church

We can make this statement because Jesus Himself revealed His future plan in a crucial discussion with His disciples that took place early in His ministry. The first time the Bible mentions a subject is very significant, and the first time the church is mentioned is on the lips of Jesus in His time with the disciples (Matthew 16:13–19) as He prophesied the church's coming. The Greek word Jesus used here is *ekklesia*, which means "called out ones." It was also used of an assembly, so the idea is that the church is a special assembly of people called out from the world to become part of God's family. This definition is critical for our understanding of the church as *people* instead of just an institution or a collection of buildings.

My purpose in looking at these familiar verses in Matthew 16 is to focus on Jesus' teaching concerning the church and the authority He gave the church to carry out His plan. Jesus had taken the disciples and traveled north for a time of retreat to get away from the crowds. It was while they were alone that Jesus raised the all-important question, "Who do people say that the Son of Man is?" (v. 13). Then He asked, more specifically, "But who do *you* say that I am?" (v. 15, italics added).

Before we get into this text, I want to point out that both of Jesus' questions (vv. 13 and 15) were directed to the Twelve as a group. It's not obvious in the English text, but the word *you* in verse 15 is plural in the Greek. This fact is important for what Jesus was about to say concerning the church.

The disciples offered several names in answer to the question of what the people at large were saying about Jesus (v. 14). His ministry did have features in common with John the Baptist, Elijah, and Jeremiah, so the people weren't completely off-base. But the important thing was who Jesus' disciples believed Him to be. So Peter stepped forward as the leader and spokesman and declared, "You are the Christ, the Son of the living God" (v. 16). The clear implication is that the other eleven disciples agreed with him. Peter was saying, "Lord, we've just been discussing this and have come to the conclusion that You are Israel's promised Messiah and Savior."

Jesus blessed Peter for this confession (v. 17), which the disciples didn't really arrive at on their own, but which came to them by revelation from God the Father. Before we go on to verse 18 and Jesus' prophecy of the church, I want you to see how important it is that the disciples were in agreement on the person of Jesus. They became the leaders and foundation stones of the church (see Ephesians 2:20). The church is a body of people who are absolutely convinced that Jesus is the one-and-only Son of God and Savior of the world.

Now we come to the heart of the passage as far as the church is concerned. In Matthew 16:18, Jesus followed up His affirmation of Peter's confession by saying, "I also say to you that you are Peter, and upon this rock I will build My church; and the gates of Hades will not overpower it."

The Church's Foundation

This is not only one of the most important statements about the church in the Bible, but also one of the most controversial. Some people teach that Peter himself is the rock on which the church is built, but that's not what Jesus said. He used a play on words here that is important to understand because it gives us the clue to Jesus' meaning.

"Peter" is the word *Petros*, a masculine form of the word for a stone. But the word *rock* that Jesus used next in Matthew 16:18 is *petra*, which is a feminine form of the same word. This word was used in classical Greek of a collection of stones knitted together to form a larger rock, such as a ledge or a slab. It meant many stones joined together to form a rock that is far larger and more significant than any one stone could be.

This is a great picture of the church. Elsewhere Paul likened it to a human body in which all the individual parts are knit together to form one whole (see 1 Corinthians 12:12; Ephesians 4:16). The analogy is different, but the point is the same. The church is not built on Peter alone, but on Peter, the other apostles, and all those who believe and confess that Jesus is "the Christ, the Son of the living God" coming together to form this larger entity called the church.

One strong support for this view is the later statement of Peter himself. Since he was there that day and heard what Jesus said, and since he obviously had access to much more teaching from the Lord that we don't have, Peter would be the best interpreter of what Jesus meant. So how did Peter describe the church in his own writings under the Holy Spirit's inspiration? He called the church "living stones [that] are being built up as a spiritual house" (1 Peter 2:5).

Let me make two observations before we go on. First, you may be saying, "But I thought the church was built on the Rock, Christ Jesus, not on Peter, the other apostles, or any other human stone."

That's true, of course, and nothing I have said above is meant to overlook or deny Jesus' ownership of His church. The church is, and always will be, the church of Jesus Christ. But it doesn't have to be either/or. Both Paul and Peter later taught that Christ was the church's one and only "corner stone" (Ephesians 2:20; 1 Peter 2:6). But Paul still referred to the apostles as the church's foundation stones, and Peter said that the church was being built out of all the stones.

A second observation I want to make concerns Peter and his key role in building the church. Jesus did address Peter directly as a central figure in the church's establishment—and, as we're about to see, the Lord went even further by committing to Peter "the keys of the kingdom of heaven" (Matthew 16:19). So, even though Christ was speaking to all of the apostles in Matthew 16, and each one had a role to play, there is no denying that Peter was the most prominent.

And yet, unlike those who want to crown Peter as the first pope who handed infallible authority and succession to others, we need to remember that Jesus said to Peter, in effect, "You are a stone. But I am not building My church on individual stones. Many stones will come together to form My church." Peter's ministry was indispensable to the church, but he was not the cornerstone.

Jesus' Promise of Victory

The last phrase of Matthew 16:18 is worthy of separate treatment because it is loaded! Jesus said, "I will build My church; and the gates of Hades will not overpower it." How do you know if the church that some leader or personality is building, or the one that you attend, is part of Jesus Christ's church? One way to know is to ask the simple question, "Who's winning?" If hell is winning, better be careful, because Jesus said His church would overcome the gates of hell.

Please notice that Jesus is on the offensive here, not the forces of Satan. Jesus is not trying to stop hell. Hell is trying to stop Jesus. A lot of ministry today has missed this point as people spend an inordinate amount of time trying to defeat the devil. But Jesus knew we could never defeat the devil on our own. That's why He came to live a perfect life, die on the cross for our sins, and be raised to life by God the Father three days later. That's why Jesus spoke of the church as yet future in Matthew 16. He had not yet been to the cross, but when He arose our Savior presented His church with a defeated Satan.

It's not that Satan and his forces won't attack and try to overcome the church. We know that our real battle is against evil spiritual forces. But Jesus guaranteed that hell will not win this battle because it has already been fought and won at the cross. Sometimes we "do church" as if we are struggling for all we're worth to be victorious. But that's not the image of the church Jesus gave us.

Jesus chose His words carefully when He spoke of the "gates" of Hades, or hell. In the biblical world, the gate of a city was the place of authority. The city's elders would sit at the city gate to conduct the city's business and render decisions on behalf of the citizens. The gate was their city hall.

Jesus was speaking of satanic authority to act against the church. God has given Satan some room to operate for now, and we are going to learn the reason for that. But the word here is that Satan's authority will not prevail against the church—which also has real implications for society at large because the invisible and spiritual world controls the visible and physical.

Thus, when the church is doing its job, all of society benefits. This is what makes the church the most important entity in the world, whether the world realizes it or not. Actually, the world will not realize the restraining and sanctifying influence of the church until God raptures His church away and *all* of hell breaks loose on the earth.

The Angelic Conflict

Jesus' statement about the gates of hell, and the reality of the battle between heaven and hell throughout the ages, brings me to the subject of what I call the angelic conflict. We need to discuss this because the church is right in the middle of this conflict that began not on earth but in heaven some time in eternity past, and will not be finished until Jesus comes and imposes on Satan his final judgment.

Your understanding of the angelic conflict is crucial to having a proper view of the church and our place in God's plan.

I'm going to summarize a lot of biblical material that you can read on your own. Two key passages you'll want to review are Isaiah 14:12–14 and Ezekiel 28:11–19. These describe an angelic being so beautiful and so awe-inspiring that he stood next to the very throne of God and directed the myriads of other angels in worshiping God. His name was "Lucifer" (Isaiah 14:12 KJV) or "light-bearer." He is called "star of the morning, son of the dawn!" (Isaiah 14:12).

We know that the angels are eternal spirit beings created by God to carry out His will and give Him the glory and the worship that He is due. The angels themselves are glorious creatures, and Lucifer was the most glorious of all. He was at the top of the angelic hierarchy. The description of him in Ezekiel 28 is nothing short of spectacular.

But at some point Lucifer fell in love with himself and decided he was tired of worshiping God. The Bible says of Lucifer, "Your heart was lifted up because of your beauty; you corrupted your wisdom by reason of your splendor" (Ezekiel 28:17). Lucifer wanted to be worshiped as God, and he convinced one-third of the angels (see Revelation 12:4) to follow him in open rebellion against God's throne. Lucifer's arrogance is summarized in the five times he declared, "I will," culminating in the boast "I will make myself like the Most High" (Isaiah 14:13–14).

But God uncovered Lucifer's rebellion and put him and the angels who followed him on trial for treason. The rebels led by Lucifer were found guilty and sentenced to eternal punishment. (Jesus said in Matthew 25:41 that hell was first prepared for the devil and his angels.) God also changed Lucifer's name to Satan, the "adversary." He became the enemy of God.

But instead of immediately throwing Satan and his demons into hell, the Bible says that the devil was "cut down to the earth" (Isaiah 14:12). For reasons that we will discuss, God banished the devil and his followers to a small speck of creation called earth. There the devil would enter into a conflict with another part of God's creation, mankind, and in the process God would be vindicated and glorified, and His power would be displayed, in an amazing way.

Satan's "arrival" on earth as his temporary realm of operation is hinted at strongly in Genesis 1:1–2, where we read that after the creation of the heavens and the earth, "the earth was formless and void." The Hebrew phrase translated "formless and void" means basically that the earth became a garbage dump.

You and I know that God doesn't create garbage. That is not only contrary to His character, but it also contradicts a clear statement in Isaiah 45:18 that the Lord "did not create [the earth] a waste place, but formed it to be inhabited." The phrase "waste place" here is the very same Hebrew phrase used in Genesis 1:2 to describe the earth as formless and void. God created the earth to be inhabited, but the earth of Genesis 1:2 was a waste place, a garbage dump not fit for habitation by mankind or any other creature.

How did the earth become a garbage dump? By becoming the domain of Satan after he was banished from heaven. God gave Satan just enough leash to reach the earth, and just enough power to exercise control over the kingdoms of this world. And any place where Satan rules becomes a wasteland.

Jesus said in Luke 10:18, "I was watching Satan fall from heaven like lightning." That lightning hit the earth, so to speak, and this planet was turned into a formless mass. When God brought order out of the chaos and prepared the earth for the creation of Adam and Eve, the devil was there in the garden of Eden to tempt them, and the angelic conflict was on.

Why did God allow Satan to set up operations on earth and wreak his havoc? The best explanation is a theological one. That is, the Godhead conferred in Trinitarian session and decreed that Satan's rebellion and judgment would be used as an opportunity to demonstrate God's power, glory, justice, and righteousness—not only to Satan and his demons themselves, but to all of creation including mankind. After all, Satan's rebellion had cast a cloud over the throne of God.

To appreciate the importance of this you have to understand

what a heinous, wicked act Satan's rebellion was. Here was the most beautiful and powerful of all God's creatures, not only rising up and shaking his fist in the face of the almighty, eternal God, but dragging one-third of God's holy angels with him—and doing so in God's perfect heaven! This was defiance, hatred, and ingratitude of monumental proportions.

Sin of this magnitude demanded more than judgment. The sinners needed to be made an example so others would see and understand and know better than to try to rebel against God.

It's like a parent whose child needs discipline. If your child disobeys you, you might sit him down for a while or send him to his room with a swat on the pants. But let's say you are a father whose son curses you and then slaps his mother in the face while the other children are watching. If that happened would you send that child to his room, or would you use the occasion to deal with him in such a way that you demonstrate beyond any doubt this had better not ever happen again?

That's the idea here. In fact, in order to demonstrate their divine power, glory, and wisdom the Godhead decided to use a creature that was far below the angels in stature to demonstrate what God can do with a lesser being who will love and obey and depend on Him—all those things that mighty Lucifer and his mighty angels refused to do.

Who is this lesser creature? Enter mankind. Hebrews 2:7 says we were created "for a little while lower than the angels." God made us this way to demonstrate to all of creation that when weak and powerless creatures like us yield ourselves to Him, neither Satan nor the angels can overpower us.

But in order to showcase His power and glory, God had to allow Satan access to us human beings so that He could prove once for all that "greater is He who is in [us] than he who is in the world" (1 John 4:4). When Satan gained access to the heart and mind of Eve and then Adam, the conflict began. But the good news is that God limited Satan's power to that of an influencer. That is, he can tempt and try to deceive, but he cannot overpower people against their will, and he is ultimately a defeated foe because of Christ.

So whenever a person is saved, the power and glory of God are on display for heaven and earth to see. Whenever a believer resists Satan's temptations and lives in victory, God's righteousness and holiness are revealed. And by the way, this issue of the angelic conflict is so important to God that when He got ready to deal Satan the decisive defeat, He didn't hurl a lightning bolt from heaven or simply crush Satan with a word. Instead, He sent His Son in the very form of that lesser creature to whip Satan face to face in the wilderness and for good on the cross. John wrote, "The Son of God appeared for this purpose, to destroy the works of the devil" (1 John 3:8).

THE KEYS OF THE KINGDOM

We've covered a lot of ground in our study of Matthew 16, but we need to go back for one verse. Jesus finished His response to Peter with these words: "I will give you the keys of the kingdom of heaven" (v. 19a).

Notice right away that Jesus did not give Peter the keys of the church. Many people today misunderstand this verse because they think that the church and the kingdom are synonymous. But Jesus was careful to distinguish the two, using a completely different word for "kingdom." This word refers not to a called-out body of believers, which is the church, but to God's comprehensive rule over all of His creation. The church is limited, whereas the kingdom is comprehensive.

Keys stand for access, so what Jesus was giving His people is access to the resources of His all-encompassing kingdom. We can be grateful that Jesus did not limit our access to the resources of the church, because the kingdom is much bigger than the church. In fact, the church exists for the kingdom and not just for the church. I say that because our job is to help establish the rule of God in the hearts of people, and bring the values and priorities of God's kingdom to bear on every aspect of our culture.

God created the church to be His agency in this age representing His bigger plan, which is the kingdom. Satan knows this, which is why he works so hard to keep churches divided. He knows that if God's people ever really get together, his influence will be severely limited.

The kingdom keys of Matthew 16:19 are plural because the gates of hell are plural. This means that for every hellish gate Satan throws open against us, there is a corresponding kingdom key that opens a kingdom door behind which are the resources we need to meet that challenge.

So every time hell tries to stop Jesus from building His church, the church is supposed to pull out its kingdom key ring and find the key that corresponds to the gate hell just opened. This is a tremendous gift from Christ to His church.

The access and authority Jesus has given to the church is also underscored by the last phrase of Matthew 16:19, where Jesus said, "And whatever you bind on earth shall have been bound in heaven, and whatever you loose on earth shall have been loosed in heaven." This is another gift from Christ, speaking of the authority the church has to carry out His agenda.

But the problem today is that too many churches are looking for power instead of authority. Over the last thirty years or so, the church has become enamored of politics. Leading evangelical figures have gained access to the halls of power.

Now please don't misunderstand. There is nothing wrong with the church seeking to impact society, but the authority we need is not found in the halls of earthly power. We've learned how easily the enemy of the church can corrupt those in positions of great political —and today, corporate—power.

Satan isn't afraid of powermongers. But he cannot stand against the authority that Christ has given the church to wield in *His* name and *His* power. The church is God's only authorized representative in the world today, so let's get busy representing our Savior and Lord.

2

THE PURPOSE OF THE CHURCH

Have you ever stopped to think about how truly amazing and unique the church is? Try to name one other organization, institution, company, government, or any entity involving human beings that is still committed to carrying out its founder's purpose and mandate *two thousand years* after it was formed!

The church is alone in that distinction, because most human organizations and power structures crumble very quickly. Alexander the Great conquered the world for the Greek empire, but within a few years of his death his kingdom was split among four of his generals. Even though the Roman Empire lasted for several hundred years, it is long gone and forgotten except in the history books.

But the church is still seeking, however imperfectly, to obey the purpose for which our Founder, Jesus Christ, established it. To state it very simply, that purpose is to be the completion of Jesus' incarnation.

That basic statement needs to be expanded and developed, which we are going to do in this chapter. But let me say up front that this does not mean Jesus' life or work on earth were incomplete in any negative sense. The idea is that He called out a people for His name to continue and complete the work He began. Now that Jesus is no longer among us in His body, the church is to be His body on earth.

Jesus made a very important declaration to His disciples the night before He was crucified. As they reclined at the Last Supper, Jesus said, "Truly, truly, I say to you, he who believes in Me, the works that I do, he will do also; and greater works than these he will do; because I go to the Father" (John 14:12). We are certainly not greater than our Lord, but we can do greater things than He did in terms of our outreach because the church has taken the gospel around the world and has brought countless numbers of people to faith in Christ. We are also able to do greater works because the Holy Spirit has come to indwell and empower each believer. This could not happen until Jesus returned to His Father (see John 16:7).

When Jesus was on earth, He limited the activity of His deity to the location of His humanity as part of His voluntary self-limitation. On at least one occasion He healed someone from a distance (see Matthew 8:5–13), but in general Jesus only ministered to people where He traveled, and He never traveled more than a couple of hundred miles from home. So in this sense, the church is doing greater works than He did.

Notice that the church is not called to do *different* works than Jesus did, only greater works. That's why I said the church's purpose is to continue and complete what Jesus began during His incarnation. I want to break this definition down into its component parts using the book of Ephesians, which perhaps more than any other book in the Bible is dedicated to explaining the mystery and the ministry of the local church. This book was not written to Christians in general but to a body of believers located in a specific place (1:1). Thus it is about the local church's visible manifestation of what is spiritually true of the universal church. Each chapter of Ephesians reveals in some way how the church is the completion of Christ and His work.

Before we get to these points, look at the way Paul introduced his subject. After an opening greeting, the apostle wrote: "Blessed be the God and Father of our Lord Jesus Christ, who has blessed us with every spiritual blessing in the heavenly places in Christ" (Ephesians 1:3). The local church is a community that has been given every spiritual gift and blessing we will ever need to carry out the work of Christ. That's important to see because Christ has not sent the church out to complete His work without equipping us completely, and even lavishly, for the job. There are at least six ways that God designed and equipped the local church to complete Christ's incarnation.

THE COMPLETION OF CHRIST'S PERSON

First of all, the church is the completion of Christ's person. Paul ended Ephesians 1 by saying that the church is "[Christ's] body, the fullness of Him who fills all in all" (v. 23). We'll back up and find out what led up to this statement, but I wanted to start here so you won't think I'm announcing heresy by implying that the Son of God is incomplete in His divine essence without us. Jesus fills all things as the Second Person of the Godhead, but Paul also said that the church is Christ's fullness.

We Are His Body

The key is to distinguish between Christ's divine essence and His functioning as the Lord of history and Head of the church. We complete His person in the way that a body completes a head by carrying out the head's orders and giving it hands and feet with which to express itself. Disembodied heads only work in horror films. Of course, Christ could have carried out His work from heaven without our help, because He is God. But He commissioned the church to finish His work after He rose from the dead and ascended back to heaven.

By the way, the body is Paul's favorite term for the church. He used it more than any other word to picture the way the church is designed to function in relation to Christ. As we said, the only job of a body is to do whatever the head tells it to do. The head is where the command center is located. If any part of your body ever disobeys the signals from your brain and starts acting independently, get yourself to a doctor right away because something is wrong. As Christ's body, the church is to move to His orders and make His presence visible as it was when Jesus was on earth Himself.

With this incredible truth before us that we are Christ's body, we can look back in Ephesians 1 and understand why Paul said, "I pray that the eyes of your heart may be enlightened, so that you will know what is the hope of His calling, what are the riches of the glory of His inheritance in the saints, and what is the surpassing greatness of His power toward us who believe" (vv. 18–19a). Paul was saying that this matter of the church is so phenomenal and so mind-boggling that if he didn't pray for them, the Ephesians might not see the full picture.

What is the full picture? Verses 19b–22 spell it out. God the Father put His surpassingly great power on display when He raised Jesus Christ from the dead and seated Him at the Father's right hand "in the heavenly places" (v. 20), and then put everything in subjection under Christ and "gave Him as head over all things to the church" (vv. 22), which brings us back to where we started in verse 23.

We need to consider a question here because it has a direct impact on the church's purpose. If God has appointed Jesus over all things, why aren't "all things" under His authority now? How can the world be in such a mess when Christ is over all?

The short answer is that the "all things" Jesus is over don't acknowledge His Lordship yet. That will happen one day when "every knee will bow" and "every tongue will confess" that Jesus is Lord (Philippians 2:10–11), because His sovereign rule extends into "the [age] to come" (Ephesians 1:21). But for now, the rest of the world does not recognize His sovereignty. This is part of God's plan, because according to verse 22 Jesus has been appointed as Head over all things "to the church" (v. 22). That means the church is the only entity on earth today that recognizes and bows to Jesus' authority.

Why is this so important? Because even though the world at large—the "all things" of Ephesians 1:22—does not bow to Christ, He is still concerned about the world. So much so, in fact, that the Bible says, "[God] is patient toward you, not wishing for any to perish but for all to come to repentance" (2 Peter 3:9). And the only way the lost world that does not recognize Christ will do so is when the church is doing its job as Christ's body, obeying His command to go into all the world to preach the gospel and make disciples of all the nations.

Peter was speaking to believers, telling them that one reason Christ was delaying His coming was so that more people could be saved. But notice that God is patient not necessarily toward sinners, but "toward you," toward Christians. In other words, God is telling us that we had better get going on the job He called us to do, because He is patiently waiting for the church to reach more people.

Everybody Is Important

When we say that the church is to complete Christ's person, it goes without saying that no local church fulfills this assignment perfectly. But each local church does have a vital role to play. The church in Paul's mind was not some amorphous concept or an ideal with no real substance. Every local church is a visible expression of the universal church, and every believer is a visible expression of Christ in his or her world.

This is why Christ's strategy for the church is so brilliant. Every time a church pronounces the benediction on Sunday and sends its people out into the world, Jesus goes out in the world with them. Jesus shows up in offices and work sites and schools all across a city because His body is there obeying His direction and making His reality visible. And when that body is multiplied around the world, Jesus shows up in His power and glory in all kinds of places all over the world. Of course, we don't do this perfectly, but that's the plan.

I want to go back to the last phrase of Ephesians 1:23, which says that the church is "the fullness of Him who fills all in all." That sounds like a tongue-twister, but it means that as we complete Christ, He completes us. As the church is faithful to be the visible, physical expression of the Lord of eternity, He will involve Himself in that process to make sure we are completing the task that He has assigned us.

But if we are going to be the visible representation of Christ to the world, that means we cannot pull out of the culture and become a private club. If Christians abandon education, the arts, or other key areas, then there is no body of Christ operating in that realm and the godless culture rushes in to fill the vacuum.

There's nothing wrong with private schools. We have a school at our church in Dallas. But we also have representatives on many public school campuses in the city, working with principals to minister to the kids. It's not either/or, but both/and.

Jesus' "Fifth Column"

During the Spanish Civil War, a communist general coined the term "fifth column" to refer to people working within a society to subvert it on behalf of their cause. This general said he had four columns of troops marching on Madrid, and a fifth column already in the city ready doing whatever it took to help topple the existing government. The term "fifth column" became a popular way to describe people who infiltrate a society, using every means at their disposal to bring down the culture for the benefit of the invading army.

The church is Jesus' fifth column. Believers are to see themselves as emissaries of God's kingdom invading the society around them to bring people under the obedience and rule of Jesus Christ. The problem we have is too many people are running around aimlessly in the church because they have never understood the church's true purpose.

THE COMPLETION OF CHRIST'S PRESENCE

As Christ's body which completes His person on earth, the church also becomes the completion of His presence on earth. These two are related because it's obvious that wherever a person's body is, that's where his presence is. In the old days students used to answer "present" when the teacher called their name on the roll. It was their way of saying, "Yes, I'm here. I am making my presence known."

That's the idea here. Jesus makes His presence known in a special way through the church. Now don't misunderstand. As the eternal God, Jesus Christ is omnipresent or present everywhere. He fills every atom of creation, so let's be clear on that. But He is uniquely present in the church, as we'll see in Ephesians 2, which is probably the greatest chapter on God's grace in the Bible.

A New Kind of Temple

I want to walk you through Ephesians 2 because it builds to a climax in verses 19–23, which is where we want to focus. This great chapter opens with us being dead in our sins and under God's wrath (vv. 1–3). But because God is full of grace, He made us alive in Christ through the grace that saves us (vv. 4–6), which is so incredible that throughout eternity we will be Exhibit A of His kindness and mercy toward lost sinners (v. 7).

That brings us to the classic statement of God's grace in salvation (vv. 8–10). But God's grace doesn't end with our individual salvation, for He has also brought all believers together in one new body, the church, which supersedes and wipes out all manmade divisions and distinctions (vv. 11–18).

That brings us to Ephesians 2:19–23, where Paul summarizes his teaching on grace by saying that God has created a new kind of temple in which His presence will dwell:

So then you are no longer strangers and aliens, but you are fellow citizens with the saints, and are of God's household, having been built on the foundation of the apostles and prophets, Christ Jesus Himself being the corner stone, in whom the whole building, being fitted together, is growing into a *holy temple* in the Lord, in whom you also are being built together into a dwelling of God in the Spirit. (italics added)

When Paul called the church a "holy temple," he was using Old Testament terminology to explain how the church is supposed to function as the expression of God's presence today. The temple in Jerusalem was the place where God was uniquely present among His people. The temple was where the special cloud of His glory appeared, and where His presence was manifested in the inner sanctum called the holy of holies.

This is why everything in Israel's life centered on the temple. Even before the permanent temple was built, the Israelites carried the tabernacle with them on their wilderness journey and set it up at the center of their camp. When the Israelites wanted to sacrifice to the Lord or worship Him, they came to the tabernacle and later to the temple. God was teaching His people that in order to enter His presence, they had to enter His temple. In the temple the people came into the presence of God's glory, were reminded of His holiness, His law, and His expectations, and had their priorities adjusted so they could go back into society and reflect His glory.

Taking Jesus' Presence Everywhere

The church is called to fulfill this function for God's people today. I'm not talking about the church as the building on the corner or down the street, although the Old Testament temple was a building. I'm talking about the church as the people of God, who are called to manifest His presence wherever we go. Yes, Christians usually gather in a building for worship, praise, and instruction in the Word, and when the church is gathered God's presence is in evidence. But we take His presence with us because the church is God's human temple. God no longer limits His presence on earth to a building made of wood and stone.

The illustration I like to use is that of America's embassies around the world. An American embassy is a little bit of America a long way from home. It is built on foreign soil, but it is a thoroughly American presence governed by American laws and values.

The church is designed to be a little bit of heaven a long way from home. We, the church, are Christ's presence on earth—the place where the values of eternity are located in time so people can see how heaven operates. The church is God's temple where His Holy Spirit dwells.

THE COMPLETION OF CHRIST'S PLAN

This is the third way in which the church completes Christ, and I love this one! According to Ephesians 3, the church is the culmination of God's plan for the ages that will demonstrate to the entire angelic realm His infinite wisdom in choosing weak vessels like us through whom to manifest His glory.

The Church Is a Surprise to Satan

Paul was explaining to the Ephesians his ministry as the one whom God called to reveal the mystery of the church. This mystery had been "hidden" for ages (Ephesians 3:9), but was now being revealed with the intent that "the manifold wisdom of God might now be made known through the church to the rulers and the authorities in the heavenly places" (v. 10).

The mention of "heavenly places" brings us back to the issue of the angelic conflict and God's plan to accomplish His will through an inferior creation called mankind. These rulers and authorities are angelic beings, which includes both the holy angels who serve God and Satan and his demons. Remember that God wanted to demonstrate what He could do with a lesser creature who would obey and follow Him.

You need to understand that this plan God set in motion to redeem fallen humanity, and call out a people for His name culminating in the church, was all a big surprise to Satan. He must have thought he outwitted God when he deceived Adam and Eve and plunged the race into sin. But Satan didn't understand what Christ was going to achieve on the cross. The devil wanted to destroy Jesus, but he didn't count on the resurrection. Paul said if the "rulers of this age" understood what God was really up to, they would not have crucified Christ (1 Corinthians 2:8).

So the church is the climax of God's plan and purpose that He set in motion in eternity past. The church is God's way of saying to the angelic realm, "This is the plan and purpose I have been carrying out on earth."

The Church Stirs the Angels

The church not only reveals to Satan and his demons how God has defeated them in Christ, but we are also the revelation of God's plan to the angels. Peter said the angels wanted to know more about God's plan of salvation and were very curious to look into it (see 1 Peter 1:12).

This is an awesome truth in itself, but it gets better. The church is not just a demonstration piece to the angelic realm. God has given us the ability to impact and stir up this realm. That's what spiritual warfare is all about. We have the Spirit and the armor of God to defeat Satan at every turn—a subject we'll deal with later.

That takes care of the demonic world, but how does the church move the angels to action? We do so by operating under the authority God has established. There's an example of this in 1 Corinthians 11:10, where we are told that when a woman is in church, "[she] ought to have a symbol of authority on her head, because of the angels." This symbol is a head covering that demonstrates that the woman accepts the authority of her husband and is operating in the proper realm.

How can this submission to authority affect the angels? Because the angels only operate under authority themselves. Jude said that even the great archangel Michael did not try to usurp the devil's realm of authority as they disputed over Moses' body (see Jude 9).

To do so would have been to violate the angelic chain of authority.

In the case of 1 Corinthians 11, the woman who refuses to operate under the authority of her husband cannot expect any angelic assistance. In other words, the angels respond when we are functioning within God's established chain of authority. God sends the angels into action on our behalf when we are operating in obedience to Him and within His established lines of authority.

This is an awesome thought. Today, only the church can get the holy angels active in history and stop Satan and the demonic world from wreaking their havoc. And, by the way, just so you won't think this is all theoretical, read Acts 12 and the story of Peter's release from prison by an angel in response to the prayers of the church in Jerusalem.

It's no wonder that Paul concluded Ephesians 3 with a doxology: "Now to Him who is able to do far more abundantly beyond all that we ask or think, according to the power that works within us, to Him be the glory in the church and in Christ Jesus to all generations forever and ever. Amen" (vv. 20–21). The church is to live for God's glory, and one way we glorify Him is to manifest His wisdom and power to the angelic realm while actually influencing that realm by our obedience to God.

THE COMPLETION OF CHRIST'S PROGRAM

Here's another facet of the church's purpose that boggles the mind. The church is to complete Christ's program by which His eternal plan is carried out in history. Ephesians 4:7–16 is a powerful passage that teaches that every believer is gifted for service and that Christ has also given the church gifted people to lead it. The Bible says, "To each one of us grace was given according to the measure of Christ's gift" (v. 7).

Christ Led a Triumphant Procession

The way Christ did this is worthy of a study all by itself. Paul used an Old Testament quotation to describe the Lord's activity prior to His ascension: "When He ascended on high, He led captive a host of captives, and He gave gifts to men" (v. 8). Then verses 9–10 are added as a parenthesis explaining what Paul meant by this intriguing statement.

This passage answers the question of what happened between the time Christ died on the cross and rose from the dead on the third day. While His physical body lay in the tomb Jesus Christ descended in His spirit into Sheol. This is the realm of the dead, which at that time was divided into a paradise side where saints went before Christ's death on the cross had fully paid for sin, and a punishment side for unbelievers (see Jesus' parable in Luke 16:19–31 for a description of this arrangement; Jude 6 also indicates that some demons are chained there).

Jesus descended into Sheol to do two things: to proclaim His victory to the demons that are locked up there, and to empty the paradise side by leading the saints there up to heaven in a triumphal procession. Paradise was moved to heaven because the temporary plan of covering sin with the blood of animals was over. The final payment for sin had been made.

Jesus Gave Gifts to the Church

In the process of completing His triumph, Jesus was authorized by the Father to hand out gifts. This is a very picturesque phrase, which was used of a Roman general who defeated his enemy and brought back the spoils of the conquered kingdom to be used for the benefit of his own land. Jesus so completely defeated Satan by His death on the cross that He was able to march into Satan's own domain and rob him of the spoils—all the redeemed saints with their gifts, talents, and abilities—which are now transferred from Satan's use to Christ's kingdom and His service.

This gifting also includes gifted leaders for the church (see Ephesians 4:11). These leaders, including pastors and teachers, have this assignment: "The equipping of the saints for the work of service, to the building up of the body of Christ" (v. 12). The church does not pay pastors to do all of the church's work, but to prepare the members of the body for their ministry. Candidates for membership at our church in Dallas cannot join unless they agree to serve in some capacity. We have well over one hundred separate ministries they can choose from, but they have to choose where they will serve.

We developed this policy to reflect our conviction that every believer has both the privilege and the responsibility to minister to the body. We don't believe people should be able to join the church and say, "Sing to me, preach to me, counsel me, encourage me, comfort me when I mourn, love and teach my children, but don't expect anything of me but to show up on Sunday morning." That's not a functioning member of the body. That's a leech.

Jesus Wants a Mature Church

The church can't operate like this because we have too big a job to do. Each part of the body has to function properly. The goal of Christ's gifting of His body is that the body might grow up into full maturity, "to the measure of the stature which belongs to the fullness of Christ" (Ephesians 4:13). The flip side of this is that we stop being an infantile body that is always fighting and fussing when someone upsets us.

Paul used another great word picture in chapter 4. As we grow up into Christ, the whole body, which is "fitted and held together by what every joint supplies, according to the proper working of each individual part, causes the growth of the body for the building up of itself in love" (v. 16).

A healthy body builds itself up and wards off disease. So when a cell decides to quit doing its assigned job and start doing its own thing, the body sends out defenders to take care of the rebel. When that doesn't happen the way it should, the result can be cancer.

It's the same way in the church. When members of Christ's body decide they don't want to cooperate with the program, they go off and start doing their own thing. That's bad enough, but these "rebel cells" want to replicate, and now you have a lump in the body. And it doesn't stop there, because that lump wants to metastasize and spread throughout the body. The result is to weaken and eventually shut the body down.

But a healthy body draws strength from every part because every part is doing its job. You and I must understand that for the church to complete Christ's program, all of the members need to function using the spiritual gifts He has given. First Corinthians 12:12–25 teaches that some gifts are exercised in public while others are more private. Some gifts are visible while others are hidden, but the church needs each person or the body of Christ will be deformed.

THE COMPLETION OF CHRIST'S PORTRAIT

We're learning a lot about the church's purpose, and it's exciting stuff. Imagine our great and awesome God entrusting the church with His climactic, all-encompassing plan and giving us the privilege of completing His Son's work.

There's a fifth way that we complete Christ, which I'm calling His portrait. When Paul discussed the relationship between wives and husbands in Ephesians 5:22–33, he said that he had a large purpose in mind: "This mystery [of a one-flesh relationship] is great; but I am speaking with reference to Christ and the church" (v. 32).

Showing What Jesus Is Like

In fact, throughout this section the apostle likened the husband-wife relationship to Christ and His bride, which is the church. The wife's responsibility is to submit to her husband's leadership the way the church submits to Christ, and the husband's responsibility is to love his wife with the selfless, sacrificial love that Christ shows to the church. Then in Ephesians 6 Paul went on to teach about the proper relationship between parents and children and employers and employees.

We can't hand someone a "portrait" of Christ and say, "This is what Christlike married couples, children, parents, or employers are supposed to look like." But God has provided a visible portrait of these relationships through the way the church is supposed to conduct its relationships. In this sense we complete Christ's portrait.

In other words, a husband is portraying Christ when he loves his wife "just as Christ also loved the church, and gave Himself up for her" (Ephesians 5:25). How much did Christ love the church? To death. So Christian husband, if you are still alive you haven't finished loving your wife yet! How long will Christ love the church? For eternity. So when can a husband quit loving and cherishing his wife? Never. This kind of love is not the feel-good stuff our culture is dishing out, but a decision to love.

And on the wife's side, we encounter the words "be subject to your own husbands, as to the Lord" (v. 22), which means submission. Many women wonder how in the world a position that seems to suggest subservience and inferiority could ever have anything to do with the faith of Christ. The answer is twofold. First, submission is often misinterpreted to mean that a woman must give up her distinct identity, gifts, and attributes to become a faceless servant. But that is worlds away from the biblical concept of submission. Second, a wife's submission to her husband reflects the submission of Jesus Christ to His Father during our Lord's earthly ministry.

We know that because of Christ Himself. When He was on earth He was completely submissive to His Father's will, even to the extent of submitting to the cross. But Jesus did not surrender any of His deity or His person to obey His Father. Christ had all the attributes of God during His earthly ministry. Submission to the Father meant that Jesus never used His attributes independently to carry out His own private agenda. He always operated in perfect concert with the Father.

A wife who submits to her husband the way the church submits to Christ doesn't lose her personhood or gifts but says to her husband, "I will use everything that God has given me not to accomplish my own program, but in concert with God's direction of you as the head of our home." That's the kind of submission that will give the world a clear portrait of Christ.

Correcting a Distorted Picture

The world desperately needs this, because all around us are distortions of what it means to be married, what a family should look like, and how relationships outside the home ought to be conducted. The reason we're having so much trouble with divorce even in the church is that we have put marriage on a sociological basis instead of a theological basis. The issue is not whether both parties in a marriage are happy, or whether they have major differences. Those things have their place, but the larger issue is that Christ has invested marriage with the role of portraying Him to the world. Marriage for Christians is a theological covenant between two people committed to making their marriage a mirror that reflects Christ and His glory.

The same can be said of our other relationships in life. People should be able to look at us in the church and see what Christ would look like and what He would do if He were a parent or a child in a family, or an employer or employee in the company downtown. The church is meant to be Christ's "family portrait," with Him in the middle.

THE COMPLETION OF CHRIST'S POWER

We're ready for the climax of this brief study of Ephesians related to the church's purpose—and what a finish it is! The church is called and equipped to complete Christ's power. Paul wrote:

> Finally, be strong in the Lord and in the strength of His might. Put on the full armor of God, so that you will be able to stand firm against the schemes of the devil. For our struggle is not against flesh and blood, but against the rulers, against the powers, against the world forces of this darkness, against the spiritual forces of wickedness in the heavenly places. (Ephesians 6:10–12)

If the church ever grasped the full reality of what God is telling us here, there would be no holding us back. Notice that we are told to "stand firm" (which is repeated twice in vv. 13–14), to stand our ground. Why didn't God tell us, "Go fight"? Because we are not fighting *for* victory, but *from* victory, and there is all the difference between those two positions. Christ has already won the victory over the devil and his schemes. Our job is to do the mop-up and hold on to the ground that Christ has already captured.

The Armor Christ Provides

So how does the local church equip its members to stand firm and complete Christ's victory? By enabling them to use the armor God has provided. These six pieces listed in verses 13–17 of Ephesians 6 are divided into two groups based on the verbs "having" (v. 14) and "taking up" or "take" (vv. 16–17). The first group is armor you have on all the time, while the second group is armor that's available nearby that you take up as needed.

For example, we need to wear the belt of truth (v. 14a) because the devil is allergic to truth. He can't stay in its presence because he is a liar. Truth is an absolute standard by which reality is measured. Truth is the absolute standard of God's Word by which everything is measured. We are not in a guessing game when it comes to what is true and what is not. Jesus said to His Father, "Your word is truth" (John 17:17).

We also help to complete Christ's power when we are wearing "the breastplate of righteousness" (v. 14b), which means a life that is consistent with the truth. I want to live the truth I preach so that my life doesn't give the lie to what I am teaching from the pulpit. None of us does that perfectly, but we should all be seeking to do it progressively as we "grow in the grace and knowledge of our Lord and Savior Jesus Christ" (2 Peter 3:18).

The third piece of armor in this "having" group is the shoes of "the gospel of peace" (v. 15). This is not referring to salvation, but to the fact that when you are walking consistently with the Lord,

He confirms your steps and helps you maintain a sure footing when the enemy attacks.

Then we come to the pieces of armor we take up as needed. This includes "the shield of faith with which you will be able to extinguish all the flaming arrows of the evil one" (Ephesians 6:16). This is a great piece of armor because the Roman shield Paul modeled this on was about four feet high and allowed the soldier to crouch behind it and protect his whole body. Paul wasn't talking about saving faith, but faith to trust God and stay true to Him when Satan hits us with his attacks.

When I read about Satan's flaming arrows I think of the old Western films in which the settlers have circled the wagons as the Indians attack. Before long Indians would be lighting arrows and shooting them into the wagons' canvas covers, and the wagons would burst into flames.

Why did the Indians do that? Because they knew the settlers couldn't fight them and the fire at the same time. The fires diverted the settlers' attention, plus if the wagons burned the settlers' protective cover would be lost. Satan takes the same strategy against us with his flaming arrows of temptation, doubt, and discouragement. But the shield of faith puts these arrows out when they land or causes them to glance off. We're safe behind the shield.

The "helmet of salvation" (Ephesians 6:17) protects your mind and refers to your identity in Christ. I'm convinced that most Christians don't know who they really are, so we have too many schizophrenic saints who are trying to live in two worlds at the same time. Most Christians still think they're nothing but sinners saved by grace. But the fact is that we are saints who sin, and that's a big difference. If we are still just sinners by nature who happen to be saved, the accent is always on our sinfulness. But if we are saints of God who bear His nature and likeness even though we still sin, the accent is on our new standing in Christ.

Paul addressed the most carnal, messed-up church in the New Testament as "those who have been sanctified in Christ Jesus, saints by calling" (1 Corinthians 1:2). The rest of this letter might make you wonder about the Corinthians' sainthood, but the first thing Paul wanted these believers to focus on was their position in Christ.

The final piece of our spiritual armor in Ephesians 6 is "the sword of the Spirit, which is the word of God" (v. 17). This is an interesting weapon because the Greek word for word here is not *logos,* the term we are most familiar with, but *rhema,* which literally means an "utterance." That's because the emphasis is not on the Word as a body of knowledge, but as a word spoken whenever the occasion demands.

We could say it's the difference between the Bible lying on your coffee table and your ability to draw on the Word in a time of need to defeat the enemy. We memorize verses and study the Bible not so we can win prizes in Sunday school, but to hide God's Word in our hearts and minds so that the Holy Spirit can bring it to our remembrance when we are toe-to-toe with the Enemy. When more Christians start treating their Bibles as a sword they need to keep sharp and ready to use, instead of a book to decorate their coffee tables, we'll see more Christians living in daily victory.

Putting on the Armor

Roman soldiers had to put their armor on in a certain order so it fit together properly and gave them the protection it was made to give. In the same way, we are to put on our spiritual armor in a definite way: "With all prayer and petition pray[ing] at all times in the Spirit" (Ephesians 6:18). You put on your armor with prayer. Prayer is the key.

Now remember that Paul is addressing the church and not just individual Christians. Prayer should be at the core of the church's ministry because that's where the power is. There is more power in prayer than there is in preaching. And yet, prayer is so anemic in most of our churches. We open and close the class or worship service with a word of prayer, and that's about it. But true prayer in the church is entering into God's presence, raising our voices as one body in one accord. Where prayer is weak, there is little true spiritual life or victory.

Jesus prayed at every turn of His earthly ministry, even with "loud crying and tears" (Hebrews 5:7). If the church is to fulfill its purpose of continuing and completing Christ's person, presence, and mission on earth, we must become people who pray as a way of life.

3

THE MISSION OF THE CHURCH

Most people in my generation grew up reciting the Pledge of Allegiance in school. We memorized it in elementary school even though we didn't understand its meaning. We repeated it throughout junior high and high school, and have spoken it many times since, with our hands over our hearts to affirm commitment to our nation and its heritage. And since 9/11, many of us have said the Pledge of Allegiance with a new sense of the responsibilities as well as the privileges of being part of this community called America.

When people come to Jesus Christ and place their faith in Him alone for salvation, they become part of something much bigger than a personal passport out of hell into heaven. The underlying purpose of this book is to help you understand that when God saved us, He placed us into a larger community, a new society called the church with certain responsibilities as well as privileges.

In fact, God the Holy Spirit took care of the "pledge of allegiance" for all believers when He baptized us into the body of Christ. Paul wrote of this new relationship, "For by one Spirit we were all baptized into one body, whether Jews or Greeks, whether slaves or free, and we were all made to drink of one Spirit" (1 Corinthians 12:13). This is not water baptism, but a sovereign ministry of the Holy Spirit whereby He places each Christian into the body of Christ at the moment of salvation. Our calling as believers is to find out how this body functions and how we are to function as its members.

Entire books have been written on the church's mission, but perhaps the most comprehensive summary of our calling is the text commonly called the Great Commission (Matthew 28:16–20). These are the last words of Jesus Christ before His ascension to heaven, which makes them crucial for that reason alone. But these are also very important words because they contain Christ's final instructions to His church, which is to "make disciples of all the nations" (v. 19).

DISCIPLE-MAKING DEFINES OUR MISSION

I want to give you two basic definitions of discipleship because it has both a personal and a corporate dimension in terms of our place in Christ's body. Discipleship is the growth process by which we as Christians learn to bring all of life under the lordship of Jesus Christ. This doesn't happen overnight, even though your salvation is complete the moment you trust Christ. Becoming a disciple means that Jesus Christ wants more of you today than He had yesterday, and He wants more of you tomorrow than He has today.

But there's more to discipleship than the personal dimension of our growth in grace. That's why I define discipleship as a *developmental process of the local church* by which Christians are brought from spiritual infancy to spiritual maturity, so that they can reporduce the process with others, which the Bible calls being "conformed to the image of [God's] Son" (Romans 8:29). This verse is crucial because it goes on to explain the goal of our becoming like Jesus Christ: "So that He would be the firstborn among many brethren."

In other words, the process of discipleship that leads to believers becoming Christlike is designed to be repeated again and again until Jesus has many brothers and sisters who look like Him. You and I can't do this if we are living as isolated Christians. Someone has said that Christianity was never meant to be "Jesus and me, under a tree." God placed us in a body of people called the church so that together we can accomplish the mission. The church is God's place to produce disciples who think and talk and act so much like Jesus that the world can look at us and say, "This must be what Jesus is like." Jesus Himself said, "It is enough for the disciple that he become like his teacher" (Matthew 10:25).

Jesus' Final Meeting

Jesus articulated the church's mission when He met with His followers in Galilee after the resurrection. Matthew 28:16 says, "The eleven disciples proceeded to Galilee, to the mountain which Jesus had designated" (see Mark 16:7). This was the only organized meeting He called during the forty days He was on earth between His resurrection and ascension. There were actually three groups at this meeting, including the eleven apostles (Judas was dead) and a second group that Paul called the "more than five hundred brethren" who saw the risen Christ at the same time (1 Corinthians 15:6).

The third group at this all-important meeting was there in spirit. This includes all believers from that day until Jesus comes again. How do I know we are part of the Great Commission meeting? Because Jesus said His commission to make disciples is in effect "even to the end of the age" (Matthew 28:20), which hasn't come yet. So the Lord's instructions are for us too.

By the way, Matthew made an amazing statement in verse 17. Some of those present with Jesus on that mountain "were doubtful" even as they worshiped Him. The Bible is clear that some of the disciples initially had a hard time buying the fact that Christ was alive again (see Luke 24:10–11). At the time of this meeting weeks later, they may have still been wondering if they were seeing a vision when He appeared to them.

But whatever the case, notice that the disciples still showed up at the meeting in Galilee. They may have been on shaky ground as to what all of this meant, but they were still willing to learn what it would take to follow Christ. You see, there are two kinds of doubt. One is the stay-at-home kind of doubt that says, "This thing will never work and there's no use even trying it."

The other kind of doubt says, "I don't understand everything that's going on here, but Jesus said to do this and I'm going to do it with His help." The doubters at the giving of the Great Commission were of the second kind, and they got to see the risen Christ.

Jesus' Declaration of Authority

Jesus' first words to His disciples in Matthew 28:18 are indispensable to the church's ability to execute its mission. I love this declaration: "All authority has been given to Me in heaven and on earth." Evans translation: "I am in charge now."

The word Jesus used for authority means "authority in legitimate hands." In other words, Jesus is not only in charge in the universe, but He is *rightfully* in charge. On September 11, 2001, our nation experienced the havoc that can be wreaked when power falls into the wrong hands. The hijackers were in charge of those four airplanes, but they stole that authority. No one granted them the right to take control. And their control lasted only until the planes crashed.

Not so with Jesus Christ. His authority was given to Him by God the Father by virtue of Christ's death and resurrection in victory over sin, death, and the devil. And Jesus is now in charge both "in heaven and on earth," in time and eternity. His authority is complete and eternal. Read the book of Revelation and you'll see that no one is ever going to unseat Him.

Jesus' Commission to Us

With His disciples worshiping Him and His authority established, Jesus gave us a commission to carry out until the end of the age: "Go therefore and make disciples of all the nations" (Matthew 28:19). Making disciples is not part of the gospel in the sense that it is not an integral part of what a person needs to know to get saved. But we need to understand that our salvation is not the be-all and end-all of what God wants to do with us. It is not the end of the process, but the beginning. Our calling isn't complete until the church is making disciples who can go and make more disciples.

We stopped our reading at verse 19 because it is the core of the commission. The phrase "make disciples" is a command in the Greek, and in fact it is the only command in this text. The other three activities—going, baptizing, and teaching—are actually participles that explain and expand the command to make disciples. (This is true even though the phrase "Go therefore" sounds like a command and is translated this way in many English versions.)

We have Jesus' authority and command to make disciples. This is exciting because it means that He is with us in the process to ensure that it works when we do it right. Here's an illustration that may help put this matter of discipleship in a familiar context.

The sermons I preach at our church in Dallas are recorded on master tapes. These masters are then put on a duplicating machine to produce audiocassette tapes for our church members and to go out all over the world through our national ministry, The Urban Alternative.

There is only one master tape for each message, but of course this master can produce any number of duplicate tapes. It's interesting that the duplicating machine into which the blank tapes are placed to receive the master tape's message is called the "slave unit." The task of the slave unit is not to create its own message, or to distort the message it is receiving, but to faithfully record and play back what is said on the master tape.

That's a picture of the discipleship process. Jesus is the Master, and we are His slaves (see Ephesians 6:6). The illustration also carries further, because the duplicate tape is never of the exact same quality as the master tape. But the goal is to reproduce the master as completely and faithfully as possible so that the correct message gets through to each listener each time one of the duplicate tapes is played.

Now don't get confused, because we are not the master. Jesus Christ is the only Master and Lord of the church, a concept we'll talk more about in the next chapter. We are the slave units, the bearers of the message. But even though we are not the master, we can put others in touch with the Master by faithfully delivering His message.

The Awesome Concept of Discipleship

I'm afraid that too many Christians have become so familiar with our spiritual jargon that we have forgotten what an awesome concept making disciples really is. Jesus committed His entire enterprise for this age to the church—to people like you and me. What's more, He told us to take it to "all the nations." Discipleship is so big that when we are obedient to God and faithful in discipling people, the church will impact the world.

How many people does it take to impact and change a nation? Not many, if they are committed enough to their cause. Again, we saw this on 9/11 when nineteen disciples of Osama bin Laden changed the face of the most powerful nation on earth. Those few committed disciples of terror sent our government scrambling to make a response that is still going on as I write these words, along with a possible reorganization of our entire intelligence community. The terrorists even forced us to expand our vocabulary with previously unheard-of terms such as "homeland security."

And America wasn't the only nation impacted by the terror attacks. Afghanistan will never be, or even look, the same. And we don't know yet all of the ways that other nations will be influenced and changed by the actions of a handful of all-out disciples. These people did not live in an advanced culture with all of the technology and firepower we possess. All they had was dogged commitment to a cause, and that allowed them to influence nations for evil.

Referring to committed members of other religions as disciples has a precedent, because the Greek word translated *disciple* in the New Testament was not a uniquely Christian term. It means "student" or learner, and the practice of making disciples was well known in the Greek world hundreds of years before Christ.

The Greek philosopher Plato developed a system of thought that bears his name. Then he trained his young disciple Aristotle in this system of Platonic philosophy. Aristotle built on Plato's teaching and developed his own system known as Aristotelian logic. Aristotle then established schools called academies to train more disciples.

This Greek discipleship system was very effective, because even after Rome conquered Greece, the Romans could not eradicate Greek influence. So while Rome wielded military power, the Greeks wielded power over the culture because well-trained Greek disciples were functioning at every level of the society. These people lived under Roman rule, but their thinking was Greek. And in the end, what people think is a lot more important and powerful than what an external power can force them to do.

This helps us understand why Jesus commissioned the church to make disciples. When it's done right, the disciple becomes a follower for life because the real battle for souls is waged in the mind. A well-trained disciple can live in a foreign, hostile culture without succumbing to that culture because his mind is fixed on another world.

There's a message here for us, because Adam handed this world over to the devil when he sinned in the garden. That's why the Bible calls Satan "the god of this world" (2 Corinthians 4:4). He will control the world's systems until Christ comes and takes them back.

But in the meantime, God has called out of the world a body of people known as the church, men and women and young people who live under the lordship of Jesus Christ. He wants us to become disciples who make other disciples, who can then be sent out into this satanically controlled world to infiltrate its structures and bring the thinking of Christ to bear on every part of society until every nation has been discipled.

Did you know that you are supposed to be a disciple on your job, bringing a kingdom worldview into that environment? That's why the church must train Christians to be in the arts and entertainment, and in politics, law, economics, and education to introduce Jesus Christ to a world that does not know Him. You don't have to be in the ministry to be called. Your calling is wherever Christ has you placed you to represent Him. That may be in your home as well as in an office or shop, because the mothers and fathers who are committed to disciple their children are shaping the next generation.

JESUS TELLS US HOW TO MAKE DISCIPLES

We've come to the final portion of the Great Commission, in which Jesus spelled out how to make disciples: "*Go* therefore and make disciples of all the nations, *baptizing* them in the name of the Father and the Son and the Holy Spirit, *teaching* them to observe all that I commanded you; and lo, I am with you always, even to the end of the age" (Matthew 28:19–20, italics added). The emphasized words are the three participles I mentioned earlier that support and expand Jesus' command to make disciples.

We Must Go to People

The first of these involves going. Let me point out again that this is not a command, but that doesn't mean our going is insignificant. On the contrary, the idea here is "As you go, make disciples." In other words, Jesus expects us to be going out. We could even say that our going is assumed.

What we are talking about is the ministry of evangelism. You can't make disciples out of sinners. The nations are not told to come to Christians for the gospel. We need to go to them. The church is not doing the work of the church if we are not winning souls to Christ. I often tell our church people that I don't want Oak Cliff Bible Fellowship to grow just by people transferring their membership. There will always be some of that growth, but I want our church to grow because we are bringing people to Christ and discipling them.

The church should be like a hospital nursery in which you hear the sound of new babies crying to be fed and eager to grow.

That's why we must keep evangelism front and center in the life of the church. If the church is going to grow by making disciples, we have to have people who are willing to go into the whole world as Christ's witnesses. That's one reason Jesus sent us the Holy Spirit. "You will receive power when the Holy Spirit has come upon you; and you shall be My witnesses . . . even to the remotest part of the earth" (Acts 1:8).

A woman in our church who was once a member of a cult and spent hours pounding the streets sharing the cult's message said to me one day, "Pastor, I went out knocking on doors when I didn't know God and didn't have the truth. So I can sure enough knock on people's doors to share Christ."

That's the spirit we need when it comes to evangelism. There is no substitute for someone going to deliver the message. A young man found that out the hard way when he decided to go into the army. He told his girlfriend he would write her every day he was away—and he did, for two years. But when he came home, he discovered she had married the mailman!

Sometimes it's hard to get Christians to go into the world with the gospel. But the cults are going out with their message, and they're not apologizing. The question is, have you gone yet?

We Must Help People Identify with Christ

Jesus said that another part of making disciples is baptizing those to whom we have gone and who have accepted Christ. He was not telling us simply to get folk wet. The problem in too many cases is that people go into baptism as dry sinners and come out as wet ones. There is much more to baptism than just undergoing a ritual involving water.

In fact, the primary meaning of the Greek word for baptism is "identification." This was a very picturesque word in New Testament days. It was used of dipping a cloth into a dye so that the cloth became completely identified with the dye by absorbing its color. The cloth was immersed in the dye until it took on the character of the dye. The cloth underwent a complete identity change.

This is the picture behind Romans 6:3–4, where Paul wrote, "Do you not know that all of us who have been baptized into Christ Jesus have been baptized into His death? Therefore we have been buried with Him through baptism into death, so that as Christ was raised from the dead through the glory of the Father, so we too might walk in newness of life."

When we put our trust in Christ, we became so completely identified with Him that His death and resurrection to new life became our death and resurrection. When we immerse believers in the waters of baptism, we are picturing their death to the old life and resurrection to a new way of life. That happened the moment they trusted Christ, but the ordinance of water baptism was given to the church as an outward testimony to this inward change.

Every believer is baptized by the Holy Spirit into the body of Christ and becomes identified with Christ and His family the church, as we learned earlier (1 Corinthians 12:13). This spiritual reality is to be made visibly manifested in history through the believer's identification and involvement with a local church body. But many Christians struggle in their daily lives because they don't understand their new identity. They don't know who they are in Christ. We have to realize that being "in Christ" is such a radically new way of life that whatever happens to Christ happens to us. That's why the Bible says that when Christ died we died, and when Christ arose from the dead we arose.

It's like putting a letter in an envelope and sealing it shut. When I do that, I don't have to ask where the letter is because the letter is safely sealed inside the envelope. So wherever the envelope goes, the letter will go too—and it's against the law for anyone but the recipient of that sealed envelope to break that seal.

Christ is the envelope, and we are the letter. We are *in Christ*. The Bible says that when you believed on Jesus Christ "you were sealed in Him with the Holy Spirit of promise" (Ephesians 1:13). How do

I know I am going to heaven? Not because I'm a preacher, but because I am in Christ and He is already seated at the right hand of the Father in heaven. I am linked with Christ forever by virtue of His grace in saving, sealing, and keeping me.

You see, your identity used to be in Adam, but not anymore. Now that you are in Christ, you have been accepted by God. You don't have to try to make God like you. So if you're on a performance treadmill in your Christian life trying to do all the right things and keep God happy with you, get off that thing and start living like someone who is identified with Christ and accepted by Him.

Did you know that all of this was tied up in the meaning of New Testament baptism? Many people equate baptism with joining a church. Church membership is important because it an act of identifying with the visible body of Christ, and many churches require their members to be baptized. But there is so much more meaning than this to baptism. When Jesus commissioned His church to baptize those who believe the gospel, He was not telling us just to make them church members. He was saying, "I want them to identify with Me so completely that My life becomes their life."

Notice also that we are to baptize people in the *name* of all three persons of the Godhead. This is a tremendous statement of both the Trinity and yet the oneness of God. Three persons are mentioned, but They share one divine name. This may be the greatest of all the mysteries of Scripture, because no one can explain the Trinity adequately. But Jesus was clear that as His commissioned followers, we go in the power and authority of the Godhead.

We Must Teach People

Once people have believed the gospel and have been identified with Christ, we must teach them "to observe all that I commanded you" (Matthew 28:20).

I'm a seminary graduate and a Bible teacher, so I can really get into this one. But teaching the nations involves more than teaching them theology, Christology, soteriology (the doctrine of salvation), and all the other "ologies" of the faith. Jesus said the goal is that people "observe" or *obey* all that He commanded us.

Of course, our teaching must have solid content, because Christians are people of the truth and people of the Book. Jesus' commands that we are to obey are contained in the Word. But the goal is not content alone. The church today has too many "spiritual bulimics" who take in the Word at church on Sunday, but then throw it up as soon as they get home so it doesn't do them any good.

The goal of biblical teaching is to combine information and knowledge with skill in applying the truth to daily life. That's why, for example, after Jesus fed four thousand people (see Mark 8:1–9), He "immediately" had His disciples get into a boat and head out (v. 10).

Why? According to Mark 8:14–21, one reason was that He wanted them to apply the lesson they had just learned about His power to meet their needs. There wasn't enough food on board for the group, and the disciples were trying to figure out what they were going to eat. So Jesus asked them some pointed questions that ended with, "Do you not yet understand?" (v. 21). Obviously they didn't, but you can be sure they thought about it for a long time and eventually the message got through. Making disciples is a process of spiritual development. It's similar to film processing, in which you take your negatives to the developer, who turns them into positives with the result that your pictures look the way they are supposed to look. God wants to take the negatives in our lives into His darkroom and turn them into positives so that we come out looking like His Son. The church and its ministry provides that darkroom where believers are brought to spiritual maturity.

Jesus Promised Us His Presence

Jesus closed the Great Commission with a tremendous promise of His presence (Matthew 28:20). The promise is made even stronger by that little word translated "lo," one of those "King James"-sounding words that we just glide over. But a more accurate translation of the phrase "lo, I" would be "I, even I," or "I Myself," because "lo" is actually another form of the first-person pronoun. As the Lord of the church, Jesus promises us His abiding presence and power to carry out His commission.

This is more than a promise of Christ's presence with us as individual believers to deal with situations in our daily lives, although of course He is always with us. This is Christ's authority given to the church to make disciples of all the nations. But to activate this promise, we have to be more than just pew-sitters or attenders when it comes to the church and its ministry.

Jesus' promise in the context of the Great Commission means that when local churches are doing what He commanded, they are going to have His presence and power in answer to prayer that they wouldn't have otherwise. They are going to have authority in ministry that isn't available to those who are not actively engaged in carrying out God's program. They are going to see God show up in ways that go beyond the normal and expected.

This promise is so incredible that if we're not seeing this kind of authority and power being exercised in the church, we need to ask ourselves why. When the church is committed to the mission of making disciples, we have Jesus' permission to use His name, His authority, His rights, and His privileges. That's all we will ever need to accomplish the church's mission.

4
THE DISTINCTIVES OF THE CHURCH

Many companies today love to talk about how their particular product or service is different from everyone else's in their field. Think of how many times you've heard lines something like these in a commercial:

> "Anyone can sell you a car [or whatever the product may be], but only our company offers you a great deal *and* great service."

> "Don't let anyone mislead you. If you want the genuine article, come to us. Anything else is second-best."

This kind of marketing is nothing new, but it seems to be gaining in popularity these days as companies have to work harder and harder to try to set themselves apart from their competition. Most

companies want to be thought of as distinctive, completely different from the crowd, a one-of-a-kind operation.

Now I'm not a marketing expert, but I can confidently state that
there is really only one entity that is totally distinctive and set apart
from everyone and everything else. No other organization except the
church has been called into being by God Himself through the
supernatural ministry of the Holy Spirit and charged with the specific task of carrying out Christ's work here on earth.

Several of the church's important distinctives are found in a
key passage that Paul wrote to Timothy, his son in the faith, fellow worker in the gospel, and the person Paul left in Ephesus
to pastor the local church there. Paul also sent Titus to oversee
the local churches on the island of Crete, which is why the books
of 1 and 2 Timothy and Titus are called the Pastoral Epistles.
These books explain what the local church is and how it works,
so we'll be spending a lot of time there in the course of this study.

In 1 Timothy 3:1–13, Paul had been instructing Timothy on the
qualifications for elders and deacons in the church. Then he said, "I
am writing these things to you, hoping to come to you before long;
but in case I am delayed, I write so that you will know how one ought
to conduct himself in the household of God, which is the church of
the living God, the pillar and support of the truth" (vv. 14–15).

It's interesting that Timothy was ministering in Ephesus, one of
the great cities in Asia Minor. Ephesus was famous for its beautiful
temple to the goddess Artemis (Diana, KJV), which was one of the
Seven Wonders of the ancient world and one of the largest temples
the Greeks ever built. The worship of Artemis was the center of life
at Ephesus, as is obvious from the Ephesians' reaction when Paul
came preaching the gospel and people started getting saved. The
apostle stirred the city up so much that the people rushed into the
arena and shouted, "Great is Artemis of the Ephesians!" for almost
two hours (Acts 19:34).

But despite this intense opposition, the church was established
in Ephesus and became a voice for the truth. Paul drew on this background in his instructions to Timothy, as we will see. His purpose

was to tell Timothy how people who belong to Christ and are part of His church ought to behave "in the household of God" (1 Timothy 3:15), which he identified as the church. Timothy knew how violently the pagans in Ephesus had conducted themselves when their goddess was threatened, but the conduct demanded of God's people who make up the church is to be entirely different. The church is distinctive in at least four important ways.

WE HAVE A DISTINCTIVE MOTIVATION

The church's first distinctive trait relates to our identity as members of God's household. The Bible uses several metaphors for the church, one of which is a family. Because God has redeemed us and adopted us into His family, we have a distinctive motivation to act right. One reason the church comes together is to learn how to live life differently under the Lordship of Jesus Christ.

We all know what it's like to try to persuade other people to act right. Some wives spend a lifetime trying to get their husbands to act right. Parents are perpetually trying to get their children to behave and stop doing this or that. But once we understand that we were dead in our sins and enemies of God before He saved us by grace and adopted us into His family, we ought to be motivated to act like the children of God.

The story is told that Queen Victoria, England's longest-reigning monarch, was eleven years old when she was told she stood next in line to the British throne. As her governess showed the future queen the list of kings and queens with her name at the bottom, Victoria burst into tears. But she quickly got hold of herself and said solemnly, "I will be good."

Victoria wanted to properly represent her royal family. How much more should we be motivated to properly represent our royal Father who is the head of our house and the King of the universe? The problem we have as believers is that when God saved us and His Spirit placed us into the church, we were saved out of the world that does not have the same value system or the same perspective on life.

So sometimes we forget who we are and who our Father is, and then we start behaving like the devil's kids again.

Most of us can remember a time when, as we were about to leave the house for some activity, our parents reminded us that we were carrying the family name and had better act right. My father often said to me, "You're an Evans, son. Act like it." It wasn't a pride thing, but an appeal to honor the family and the Lord by my behavior so that I would not bring shame.

We are members of God's household, His children, whom Christ purchased with His own blood. Talk about something to motivate a person to right conduct! No one else on earth is offering the deal God is offering folk through His body the church. Instead of constantly telling Christians that they need to stop doing wrong and start doing right, we need to help them understand who they are in Christ. That doesn't mean there won't be problems, but understanding our identity in Christ is a far higher motivation for right conduct than just the fear of messing up.

Our motivation is also affected by the people we hang out with. Most Christians spend far more time with non-Christians than they do with God's family, in terms of their everyday environment as opposed to the few hours a week they spend in church. That's fine, because we are supposed to be salt and light. The problem comes when the influence works the other way—when Christians start talking and acting like the devil's kids. This also applies to the things we watch, read, and listen to every day.

If we want to be demotivated in a hurry, we can start absorbing the values and attitudes of people, television programs, films, or anything else that does not reflect the value system and behavioral standards of God's family. When this happens, then we start saying and doing things we wouldn't normally do, even though we know we didn't learn them from our Father and they don't belong in His house.

Paul's prayer for the Colossians gives us a succinct statement of the motivation we need to have. He told these believers that he never stopped praying for them, "that you may be filled with the knowledge of [God's] will in all spiritual wisdom and understanding, so that you will walk in a manner worthy of the Lord, to please Him in all respects" (Colossians 1:9–10).

WE HAVE A DISTINCTIVE MASTER

"The household of God, which is the church of the living God" (1 Timothy 3:15) not only has a distinctive motivation. We also have a distinctive Master—God Himself in the Person of Jesus Christ. The Bible leaves no doubt as to who is in charge in this house. Make sure all the family knows who is the Master of the church, because the church is God's assembly. It's a divine institution. Let the family of God know who the head of the house is, lest we start doing what a lot of teenagers do and insist on living by our own rules while we're living in someone else's house.

Nothing is more upsetting to a home than a teenager who wants to live by his own standards and ignore the rules of the house. How many parents have said to their teens, "If you want to make up your own rules, get your own house. But if you want to live in this house, you're going to have to live on our terms, because we're paying the bills."

A father once told his teenage son to turn the volume down on the music he was playing in his room, but the boy hit his dad with this familiar line: "I can do whatever I want in my room!" The dad didn't get mad and holler back. He just got out his house note, showed his son whose name was on it, and said, "You're wrong, Son. I don't see your name anywhere here. This is my room in my house that I let you sleep in."

The church is God's house, not ours. My job as a pastor is not to make up the rules for the church, but to announce and teach God's rules outlined in His Word. His name is on the title deed to the church, because "He purchased [it] with His own blood" (Acts 20:28). When the risen Christ appeared to His disciples, "He showed them both His hands and His side" (John 20:20). These are the marks of His ownership.

When I was growing up, we played football all year round. And like most boys, I liked being the quarterback because he was the one in charge who got to call the plays. But when we went out to the sandlot to play a game, we never knew who was going to show up. There could be some guys there who were bigger and older than me, and of course whoever was the biggest or the oldest got to choose his position first.

But I quickly figured out that whoever brought the football got to call the shots, so I tried to make sure I was the one who brought the ball. That way I could be sure I got to be the quarterback. God owns the ball, so He gets to call the shots for the church. One thing that makes the church distinct from all other entities is our distinctive Master.

Now don't misunderstand. God is the Master of the entire universe. "The earth is the Lord's, and all it contains, the world, and those who dwell in it" (Psalm 24:1). There is no one or nothing under heaven beyond God's control, even though most of the world does not acknowledge that fact. When Jesus returns to reign over this earth, every part of creation will bow to His Lordship, but until then God is the recognized Master of the church.

Speaking of relationships, Paul's reference to the church as a household is important because believers are to relate to one another as family. Later in 1 Timothy, the apostle instructed Timothy: "Do not sharply rebuke an older man, but rather appeal to him as a father, to the younger men as brothers, the older women as mothers, and the younger women as sisters, in all purity" (5:1–2).

One reason this is important is that the church is not just another organization with structures and rules, but a living, breathing family in which we relate to one another as brothers, sisters, fathers, and mothers. That's why it's very appropriate for Christians to refer to their church as their family. We encourage the people in our church in Dallas to use family talk in reference to one another.

The church is God's household, and He is the Master of the house. I love the response of the young boy Samuel, who was living in the temple when God called to him one night. When he heard God calling his name, Samuel said, "Speak, for Your servant is listening" (1 Samuel 3:10). This is the attitude of obedience we need to have when our Master speaks to us today.

WE HAVE A DISTINCTIVE MISSION

You would expect a living body with a distinctive motivation and Master to have a distinctive mission, and that's what we find with the church. Paul pointed to this mission when he told Timothy that the church is "the pillar and support of the truth" (1 Timothy 3:15).

We Are to Hold up the Truth

I said earlier that Paul drew on the religious background of Ephesus to help deliver his message. This is a case in point. Picturing the church as a pillar that helps to support a structure would have had vivid meaning to the people of Ephesus, because one notable feature of Artemis's fabulous temple was its lavishly decorated pillars. There were more than a hundred of these pillars supporting the temple, with all kinds of decorations on them in honor of various gods who supposedly joined the people in paying homage to the great Artemis.

The problem was that the pillars in the temple of Artemis helped hold up a lie because Artemis was not the true God. There is only one source of truth in the universe, which Paul said elsewhere is found "in Jesus" (Ephesians 4:21). And since Jesus has entrusted His Word of truth to the church, the church is to be the guardian and disseminator of the truth. No other body of people on earth has been given this assignment to uphold truth.

In later chapters we will get into the specifics of the church's mission as it relates to things like worship, fellowship, proclamation, and evangelism. But in all of these activities, the overarching mission of the church is to verbally and visibly testify to the truth of the one true God. We as the people of God who have been united by Christ into one body are called to proclaim and live out the truth.

Pontius Pilate cynically asked Jesus, "What is truth?" (John 18:38). Jesus did not reply at that moment, but earlier in the Upper Room with the disciples He had declared, "I am the way, and the truth, and the life" (John 14:6). And in His prayer to the Father on behalf of those who believed in Him, Jesus said, "Sanctify them in the truth; Your word is truth" (John 17:17).

Truth is simply a fixed standard by which reality is measured, a non-negotiable reality. It is that which corresponds to the facts. Once you lose truth, you lose even the possibility of measuring or evaluating anything with any degree of accuracy. Once you lose truth, you also lose freedom. Remember that Jesus said, "You will know the truth, and the truth will make you free" (John 8:32).

The corollary of that principle is also true. Lies lead to bondage, which explains why the unsaved world is in bondage to Satan, who is "a liar and the father of lies" (John 8:44). Those who serve as a pillar and support of lies become slaves to those lies.

Truth is the only way to freedom even when that truth may be painful or inconvenient or lead to a struggle. The church's mission as a truth-teller cannot be compromised without leading people into error and eventual bondage to the lies of Satan.

It's worth noting that even on the political scene, truth and lies produce the same results. For instance, wherever there is political and social freedom we usually find that the press and other social organs are free to say what they want, even if they are critical of the government. One of the first things an oppressive regime has to do is gain control of the media so the leaders can tightly control what people know and issue propaganda to undergird their lies. Every dictator knows that it's absolutely vital to restrict what the people hear and read so that the only information they get is the "party line." Lies told often enough and skillfully enough can keep people locked away behind iron and bamboo curtains just as effectively as behind soldiers and barbed wire.

That's why one of the first things that often goes into operation in a dictatorship is the so-called underground press whose purpose is to give the people an alternative view and counter the endless official lies of the regime. The people who operate an underground press at the risk of their lives understand that truth can be as powerful as armed resistance in bringing down a regime that depends on lies for its support.

It's true that having a free press does not protect a society from excesses. We're seeing plenty of excesses in our own culture as people are allowed to say whatever they want without regard for good taste, let alone the truth. But truth is powerful enough to compete in the marketplace of ideas. It's like a lion, who just needs to be turned loose and he'll take care of himself.

We Are to Proclaim the Truth

The church simply needs to convey God's truth in all of its clarity and power. Yes, we must also defend the truth from distortion and misrepresentation, but the best defense of truth is a good offense in which we are taking God's Word to the ends of the earth. Jesus said, "I am truth," not "I know the truth" or "I have access to the truth." He is the personification and embodiment of all that is true, so when we proclaim Him to the world we are giving people a sure standard against which to measure and judge all reality. Therefore, anything that does not line up to Jesus is false.

The church is distinctive in its message because we are obligated to proclaim the truth even when no one else agrees or stands with us. Our society only wants convenient, comfortable truth that fits with people's preconceived ideas and biases. If things continue going the way they are, the church may well be the only place left on earth where the next generation can get the real story on the way things are.

That means the church had better be doing a good job of upholding and imparting the truth. One way we do that is by learning and knowing the Word of God. You can't uphold or teach what you don't know. Paul exhorted Timothy, "Be diligent to present yourself approved to God as a workman who does not need to be ashamed, accurately handling the word of truth" (2 Timothy 2:15). We need to learn the truth before we can impart it to someone else.

We Are to Live out the Truth

But along with learning goes the need to live the truth. In another of his pastoral epistles, Paul urged Titus, "Speak the things which are fitting for sound doctrine" (2:1). The following verses reveal why it was so important for Titus to teach sound doctrine. God was interested in the way the believers on Crete lived their lives. The goal of Titus's instruction was that Christians would "[show] all good faith so that they will adorn the doctrine of God our Savior in every respect" (v. 10).

To adorn means to decorate or dress something up in a way that makes it look nice and people are attracted to it. Local churches are to teach their members to "wear" God's truth by putting it on display in our daily lives. It's true that not everyone is looking for the truth, but many people will be attracted to believers whose lives correspond to truth.

Notice the Bible says we need to wear our doctrine, not wear it on our sleeves. We've all known Christians who seem to be itching for a chance to let unbelievers have it with both barrels, or who are ready to argue at a moment's notice. There's nothing wrong with defending the truth, but taking a "holier than thou" stance or letting everyone know that we don't do this or that is not the kind of adornment of truth the Bible has in mind. People were attracted to the believers in the early church and came to see what was going on because their lives radiated Christ.

The gospel is "the power of God for salvation to everyone who believes" (Romans 1:16). Like the lion we mentioned earlier, God's Word will do its work in hearts if we simply proclaim it accurately and faithfully. And when our own lives line up with the truth, our message has even more impact because we become Exhibit A of what God can do.

WE HAVE A DISTINCTIVE MESSAGE

The church's fourth and final distinctive in 1 Timothy 3 is our distinctive message. "By common confession, great is the mystery of godliness," Paul began in verse 16. Again, this was a play on the worship of Artemis, because her followers in Ephesus used to chant, "Great is Artemis of the Ephesians."

We Have a Great Mystery to Explain

The church's message is great too, summarized here as "the mystery of godliness." In the Bible, a mystery is not a puzzle or dilemma that no one can figure out, but a truth previously hidden that has now been revealed. The mystery that the church has been called to uphold and proclaim is all about the person and work of Christ, as the rest of verse 16 makes clear.

Most Bible teachers believe that the remainder of this verse was an early hymn that the church learned and recited to remind themselves of the truth. Notice that each line or stanza of this hymn is about Jesus. He *is* the mystery of God, "He who was revealed in the flesh, was vindicated in the Spirit, seen by angels, proclaimed among the nations, believed on in the world, taken up in glory."

The church's message is Jesus from beginning to end. That's the only thing that makes us distinctive from any other body of people. Everything else we teach and do has to grow out of that central focus, or we'll get off track. The reason so many churches are not having the impact they should be having for Christ today is that they are all tied up doing peripheral things while neglecting the core of the church's life, which is Jesus Christ.

When the church has nothing to offer the world but the same basic message as a political party or some other entity, we lose our distinctiveness. Paul said, "We preach Christ crucified" (1 Corinthians 1:23). That's the church's mission in five words or less, so let's look at what this great early church hymn in 1 Timothy 3:16 says about our distinctive Lord and our distinctive message.

We Have a Great Savior to Proclaim

First, in 1 Timothy 3:16, Jesus was "revealed in the flesh." That's very important, because it does not say that Jesus originated in the flesh. He simply became visible in the flesh when He was born of the virgin Mary, but Jesus existed before His birthday. We call His conception and birth the Incarnation because in it God took on human flesh. Isaiah said of the Messiah that a child would be born, but a Son would be given (see Isaiah 9:6). The child born in the manger of Bethlehem was already the Son of God. "The Word became flesh, and dwelt among us" (John 1:14).

Jesus was not only supernaturally conceived, but He lived a supernatural life here on earth. The next line of Paul's hymn says that Jesus "was vindicated in the Spirit." Everything Jesus did and every claim He made was vindicated or proven true by the Holy Spirit's power at work in His life. Jesus demonstrated Himself to be super-natural in at least three ways.

First, our Savior lived a perfect, sinless life. One day as He was being grilled and accused by His enemies, Jesus said to them, "Which one of you convicts Me of sin?" (John 8:46). There was no answer, because no one had anything on Him. According to Hebrews 4:15, Jesus experienced every temptation we will ever face, yet He did so "without sin." You have to be supernatural to live a sinless life, and Jesus is the only person who has ever done it.

A second way that Christ showed Himself to be supernatural was by miracles He performed. No one can be raising folk from the dead, walking on water, and healing the blind, the sick, and the lame with-out supernatural power. Jesus said to His disciples at the Last Sup-per, "Believe Me that I am in the Father and the Father is in Me; otherwise believe because of the works themselves" (John 14:11).

The third and greatest vindication of all in Jesus' earthly life was His resurrection. Paul said that Jesus "was raised because of our justification" (Romans 4:25). The reason we know that Jesus' claim to forgive our sins by His death on the cross is real is that He got up out of the grave. The resurrection is our "receipt" of the sal-vation that Jesus purchased for us on the cross, and it vindicated His claim to be the Son of God.

The next declaration in the hymn of 1 Timothy 3:16 is that Jesus was "seen by angels." Angels were active at every important stage of Jesus' life. An angel foretold His birth, a whole choir of angels showed up at His birth, and angels guided Joseph at crucial points in the birth and early life of Jesus. Angels ministered to Jesus when He was tempted in the wilderness and on the cross. Angels were also there at the tomb to roll the stone away and announce His resurrection, and when Jesus returns the angels will be with Him.

In other words, heaven endorsed Jesus throughout His life. And the demons, the angels who followed Satan in his rebellion and were kicked out of heaven, were scared to death of Jesus. Let me tell you something. The holy angels aren't awed by ordinary humans like you and me, and demons aren't afraid of us. It takes the God-Man to make the good angels bow and worship and the bad angels shake with fear. James said, "The demons also believe, and shudder" (James 2:19).

There are three more statements or stanzas to this hymn of Paul's we're studying that captures the essence of the church's distinctive message. The next one is that Jesus was "proclaimed among the nations." This is another way of stating the Great Commission that Jesus Himself gave us, in which He told us to make disciples of all the nations.

Let's stop here for a minute and use a little bit of "Holy Ghost" logic on this statement. Jesus told His followers to take the gospel into the whole world, and they have done so, even in the face of persecution and death, because they were convinced that He was indeed the Son of God who had risen from the dead. But if Jesus was not risen, it makes no sense that otherwise sane people would go out and enthusiastically give their lives for something they knew wasn't true. I don't know too many people who are willing to risk their lives for a dead man and a lost cause.

During the carnage at the Battle of Gettysburg in the Civil War, the Confederate forces who made the ill-fated "Pickett's charge" on the Union lines were being cut to ribbons as they moved forward. At one point the Confederates encountered a fence that they had to stop and cross while undergoing intense enemy fire. As the troops took cover and realized the absolute futility of the attack, a number of the men simply turned around and headed back toward their own lines. It wasn't a matter of desertion or cowardice. They just realized that they were heading into certain death on a hopeless mission.

The disciples of Jesus charged straight into the guns of the world because they had seen the risen Lord and knew that He was alive. They went out to proclaim Him among the nations, and now it is our turn to take up the mission.

When Jesus is proclaimed, the truth of the next stanza of 1 Timothy 3:16 follows. The Bible says that He is "believed on in the world." This is what we've been saying, that when the church presents the message of Christ in the power of the Holy Spirit, people will respond. People today are dying for something to believe in, and we have a unique Word to present about a unique Person.

Paul ended this great statement of faith by saying that Jesus Christ was "taken up in glory." This was His ascension, when He went up in the sight of the disciples and was lifted back to heaven (see Acts 1:9–11). Jesus' ascension was bodily, not just a spirit. He will also return bodily, because the angels at His ascension told the watching disciples, "This Jesus, who has been taken up from you into heaven, will come in just the same way as you have watched Him go into heaven" (Acts 1:11). Jesus is the distinct and unique message of the church. An old church in England had this sign on it: "We preach Christ crucified." But as time went on, some ivy began to grow over the sign and obscure part of it. Soon the only part of the sign that could be seen was, "We preach Christ." The ivy continued to grow, and before long the sign said, "We preach." But then even the word "preach" was blocked out, and all that was left was the word "We."

Unfortunately, what happened to the sign also told the story of what happened to this church. It began to surrender its calling of preaching Christ crucified, and the church began to die. By the time the sign out front showed just the one word "We," the church was a dark, empty building.

When all that a church has left is "We," that church is in trouble. For like a boxcar that has been disconnected from its train, when the church gets disconnected from Christ it isn't going anywhere. Let's make sure that the church does not surrender its distinctive motivation, Master, mission, and message.

5
THE POWER OF THE CHURCH

If you have ever read a great book and then heard the author speak, you know how that encounter with a living person who knows the whole story can make a book come alive in a new and richer way. A large auditorium full of people in Dallas had that experience some years ago when Alex Haley, the author of the well-known book *Roots*, came to town as part of a local university's distinguished lecture series.

Roots, which is Haley's account of his family's history from slavery in the 1700s to his own day, had already become a classic by this time. And that evening, as Haley told about being a young boy who sat on the porch on summer nights listening through the screen to his mother and aunts tell the stories of their ancestors, his audience was spellbound. A friend of mine who was there said Haley's description was so vivid he could almost feel the summer breezes blowing on the porch and hear the women inside laughing as they talked.

That's the kind of power that an author can bring to his or her work. Although human illustrations ultimately fail to fully convey divine reality when it comes to the person and work of God, what Alex Haley did for his audience that night in Dallas is similar to what the Holy Spirit does for the church when He applies the Word of God to the hearts and minds of His people and energizes us for a life of godliness and service.

The Holy Spirit is the power of the church, in the same way that the engine in a car supplies the power to make the car go. Without this power source the church may look good, like a new car sitting in the parking lot. But we won't get anywhere. That's because living the Christian life without the active participation of the Holy Spirit is impossible. It is possible to know the Bible and not know the Lord, to memorize Bible verses and yet not be transformed, because only the Holy Spirit can make what is true in the Bible become real for you and me.

It is also impossible for the church to be the church that God intended us to be apart from the dynamic ministry of the Holy Spirit. That's because Jesus said, "Apart from Me you can do nothing" (John 15:5), and Jesus is the One who sent the Spirit to indwell and empower the church.

THE HOLY SPIRIT WAS PROMISED TO THE CHURCH

It was Jesus Himself who alerted us to the absolutely critical role that the Holy Spirit was to play in the church, and it was Jesus who promised to send the Spirit after His ascension back to the Father. On the night before His crucifixion, Jesus told the disciples, "I tell you the truth, it is to your advantage that I go away; for if I do not go away, the Helper will not come to you; but if I go, I will send Him to you" (John 16:7).

The Promised Spirit of Truth

Jesus then referred to the Spirit as "the Spirit of truth . . . [who] will guide you into all the truth" (v. 13). This is key to the Spirit's ministry since we have already seen that His basic job is to make God's truth come alive within us.

We could use many analogies for this process. The Spirit's work is like taking the still photographs of the Bible and turning them into a motion picture in our lives. Of course, the Bible is living and true and powerful whether we believe it or not. But the Word will lie dormant until the Holy Spirit comes and makes dead people alive and then plants the truth in their hearts.

If you could have taken a vote among the disciples at the Last Supper as to whether they thought it was a good idea for Jesus to leave them, the outcome would have been 11–0, not counting Judas. They didn't want Jesus to leave. They were upset and distressed when He told them He had to leave (see John 16:5–6). And if you asked many believers today which would be better for the church, to have Jesus among us in person or have the Holy Spirit indwelling us, you would probably get a lot of votes for the first option.

But we are better off with the Spirit than we would be if Jesus were here in the flesh, for reasons we discussed in a previous chapter. Jesus limited Himself in the flesh, but the Spirit pervades and invades every place and permanently indwells every believer (see John 14:17b) because He is the omnipresent God, the third Person of the Trinity.

The Promised Spirit of Power

In fact, Jesus also indicated that no Spirit equals no power. Just before His ascension, the Lord made another great promise to His apostles: "You will receive power when the Holy Spirit has come upon you; and you shall be My witnesses both in Jerusalem, and in all Judea and Samaria, and even to the remotest part of the earth" (Acts 1:8). This promise was fulfilled just a matter of days later at the birth of the church in Acts 2, which we'll deal with later.

Think about what Jesus' promise really meant. The apostles had spent more than three years listening to Jesus teach and watching Him work. They had spent three-plus years absorbing truth from the eternal Son of God, who was preparing them to be foundation stones in His church (see Ephesians 2:19–20). Peter and the other apostles were not lacking for information to do what God wanted them to do.

But Jesus knew they were lacking in power. And even though He had been their Bible teacher, He told them that they wouldn't have power until the Holy Spirit came. According to Acts 1:4–5, Jesus prefaced His promise by telling the disciples not to leave Jerusalem until the promised Spirit had been given. Otherwise, all that they had learned wouldn't work. So their main job at that point was to wait for the Holy Spirit to show up.

The disciples did that, and then we read in Acts 2,

> When the day of Pentecost had come, they were all together in one place. And suddenly there came from heaven a noise like a violent rushing wind, and it filled the whole house where they were sitting. And there appeared to them tongues as of fire distributing themselves, and they rested on each one of them. And they were all filled with the Holy Spirit and began to speak with other tongues, as the Spirit was giving them utterance. (vv. 1–4)

Pentecost was the church's birthday, and it was the power and activity of the Holy Spirit that brought the church into being. We are going to spend a good portion of this chapter talking about what it means to be filled with the Spirit, which is the secret of where the church's power lies. The Spirit's presence was manifested as wind and fire, a powerful invasion from heaven that the disciples had never known before.

When the Holy Spirit came with power, the disciples were able to speak in a way they had never been able to speak before, declaring the message of God in a number of languages they hadn't learned (Acts 2:5–11). They were able to do things they had never done before because they were filled with the Holy Spirit.

What we are missing in the church today is not programs and seminars and information. We are missing the Spirit's power that comes from His filling. The more Spirit-filled Christians you have, the fewer programs you need. The church's job is not to replace the Spirit's ministry with other things, even good things. Having everything in place and being organized is fine, but we have to make sure that we don't organize ourselves out of our need for the Spirit. Sound Bible teaching is critically important for imparting truth, and helping us discern the true from the false when it comes to the claims people make in the spiritual realm. But Bible teaching by itself cannot substitute for the Holy Spirit's presence. Teaching is a prelude to the supernatural.

When Jesus' promise of the Spirit's coming was fulfilled, something supernatural from heaven occurred. The rest of the book of Acts is a proof of Jesus' statement to the disciples that they would receive power when, and only when, the Holy Spirit came and filled them. Acts is about what the local church looks like when the Holy Spirit takes over. The greatest thing that can be said about any church is that it is filled with people who are full of the Holy Spirit.

THE SPIRIT IS ACTIVE IN THE CHURCH

Since the Day of Pentecost the church as the people of God has been indwelt and energized by the Holy Spirit. I want to look briefly at several of the Spirit's distinct ministries to and through the church as they relate to our thesis, which the Bible clearly teaches, that the church's power resides in the Holy Spirit's person and work.

The Spirit Indwells Us

There is no saved member of the church of Jesus Christ who does not have the Holy Spirit living inside him or her. When the Spirit takes up residence in your life, He will never leave you. Jesus said of the Spirit's coming, "He . . . will be in you" (John 14:17). The Holy

Spirit baptizes every believer into the body of Christ at the moment of salvation (see 1 Corinthians 12:13).

We know that every Christian is indwelt by the Spirit because Paul said, "You are not in the flesh but in the Spirit, if indeed the Spirit of God dwells in you. But if anyone does not have the Spirit of Christ, he does not belong to Him" (Romans 8:9). The Spirit's abiding presence in the people of God who make up the church gives us the continual access to His power that we need to pull off what God has called us to do.

The Spirit Is Our Teacher

This is one of the Holy Spirit's most crucial, and yet too often overlooked or undervalued, ministries to the church. The Spirit is the church's divine Teacher. We alluded to this above when we said that the Spirit's job is to take the Word of God and bring it alive in our lives.

During His discourse in the Upper Room before the crucifixion, Jesus referred to the Spirit's future teaching ministry. "The Holy Spirit, whom the Father will send in My name, He will teach you all things, and bring to your remembrance all that I said to you" (John 14:26). And again, "When He, the Spirit of truth, comes, He will guide you into all the truth" (John 16:13). If you want to know the Word of God in all its power, you need God's Spirit for your Teacher.

Let me explain why I think the Spirit's teaching ministry is so often overlooked. It's because too many of us think that all we have to do is accumulate Bible knowledge and go out and put it into practice, the way a dad might follow the assembly manual to put his child's bicycle together on Christmas Eve. It's just a matter of following the steps, studying the illustrations, and picking up the right part at the right time.

But the Christian life isn't an assembly manual. Paul said something very eye-opening in 2 Corinthians 3:6: "The letter kills, but the Spirit gives life." Paul was referring specifically to the law of

Moses, which in itself could not give life because it carried no power to help anyone obey. That power only comes from the Spirit.

But the principle Paul stated in this verse applies to what we are talking about here. You can actually go to church and listen to Bible teaching, and study the Word for yourself, and yet be worse off for it spiritually.

Let me illustrate what I mean. I attended one of the greatest seminaries in the world and studied under some of the finest professors and Bible teachers available anywhere. When I entered seminary I was full of excitement and enthusiasm at the thought of learning the Bible from these great teachers. And I did learn, studying the Bible and its related subjects from morning till night.

But anyone who has studied the Bible in an academic environment can tell you how easy it is to go from learning God's Word so that it can change and shape your life to learning it as information to be digested and memorized so you can pass a test and earn a degree. When that happens, you begin to grow weaker and more mechanical in your faith and your walk with God even as you're learning more about Him.

That happened to me to some extent during my seminary years. In other words, I began to grow cold spiritually. It wasn't because I was not learning the truth. It wasn't the professors' fault, because they were godly men whose teaching was marked by the Spirit's power. The problem was that I got so wrapped up in what I was learning that I stopped applying and living what I was learning. I was learning from my teachers, but I wasn't learning from *the* Teacher, the Holy Spirit. Knowledge for its own sake is not His goal. He wants us to be transformed by the truth.

Now, don't misunderstand. We need to know the Bible, because the Holy Spirit only teaches and applies the Word. He is not interested in applying our philosophy or human reasoning. But the "letter" of the Word without the Spirit kills instead of bringing life.

Jesus made a very interesting statement in John 5:39–40 as He was dealing with those who sought to kill Him (see v. 18). The Lord said, "You search the Scriptures because you think that in them you have eternal life; it is these that testify about Me; and you are unwilling to come to Me so that you may have life."

If these people were searching the Scriptures, why wasn't their search leading them to believe in Jesus and find eternal life? One answer is that those who rejected Jesus refused the Holy Spirit's ministry of enlightenment and conviction of the truth. Jesus' worst enemies, the Pharisees, were what we would call the Bible scholars of the day. They read the Old Testament constantly, but their study led them away from rather than to the Messiah. These learned men and their followers had all the right information, but they experienced no transformation because they refused to allow the Holy Spirit to apply His teaching and convicting ministry.

The Spirit Equips Us for Ministry

There is one more activity of the Holy Spirit related to the church that I want to point out before we turn to the Spirit's filling. The Bible teaches that the Holy Spirit is the source of the spiritual gifts that make it possible for the church to execute its ministry.

The apostle Paul wrote to the Corinthians concerning spiritual gifts, "Now there are varieties of gifts, but the same Spirit" (1 Corinthians 12:4). Going on to verse 7 we read, "But to each one is given the manifestation of the Spirit for the common good." And then after mentioning a number of gifts, Paul clinched his point that the Holy Spirit is sovereignly in charge of the gifts: "But one and the same Spirit works all these things, distributing to each one individually just as He wills" (v. 11).

People get all worked up today arguing about the gifts—which ones are still in effect and how we should think about those who claim to have the more spectacular gifts like healing and tongues. This is not the place for that discussion, but whatever your view is, the point I want us to see is that the power is not in the gift or the person exercising it, but in the Holy Spirit who gives the gift. The Bible's emphasis is in the place where ours needs to be, on the Giver rather than on the gift or the recipient.

THE SPIRIT FILLS THE CHURCH

Now we come to that portion of the Holy Spirit's ministry where I want to do some extended study. The Bible says, "Do not get drunk with wine, for that is dissipation, but be filled with the Spirit" (Ephesians 5:18). This command is written in the plural, which means it is addressed to the whole church. More than that, it is a conditional command that requires us to continually be filled with the Spirit on an ongoing basis because the filling can be lost.

When we say that the Holy Spirit fills the church, we mean of course the believers who make up the church—both individually and in our corporate life when we come together as the body of Christ. The Holy Spirit's filling is commanded for every Christian, because the Word of God is designed to lead us to experience His supernatural power for holy living and ministry.

The Necessity of the Spirit's Filling

If this is true, we need to ask why more of us are not experiencing the supernatural—and by this I don't mean the spectacular stuff, but such an obvious power of God in our lives and in our churches that no natural explanation for what's happening will suffice. The short answer is that individual Christians and churches are not Spirit-filled. Why are more churches not seeing the supernatural power of God at work in their midst? Because they are not Spirit-filled churches made up of Spirit-filled people.

They may be Bible-teaching churches with great programs, and thank God for that. But unless the Holy Spirit is filling the people on the platform and in the pews, the result will ultimately be church as usual. I don't know about you, but I don't want to settle for the usual. I want to see God's wind and fire sweep through His church as He fills us with Himself through the work of the Spirit.

You may be saying, "Tony, you just said that all true Christians have the Holy Spirit living inside of them all the time. Now you're saying we need to be filled with the Spirit. Don't we already have all of the Spirit within us?"

Yes we do, if we are talking about the Spirit's indwelling. The Bible says that God "gives the Spirit without measure" (John 3:34). But the Spirit's filling is different than His indwelling. We are never commanded to be indwelt by the Spirit, but we are commanded to be filled. The indwelling is permanent and unconditional, while the filling is not permanent in the sense of happening once for all, but is conditional.

The word *filled* means "to come under the control of." That should give us a clue to the difference between indwelling and filling. The issue in filling is not how much of the Spirit we have, but how much of us the Spirit has. We need to be filled with the Spirit for the same reason we need to stop at a gas station if we plan to drive somewhere. We need fuel to energize the motor in our car.

You don't need to get a new engine when you pull into a gas station. You just need to be filled with fuel or you're not going to get very far. That's why the Spirit's filling is so important to the church.

The Renewal of the Spirit's Filling

To carry this analogy a step further, the moment you leave the gas station and start driving, what happens? You begin using up the fuel in your tank, and at some point you will have to stop again for refueling. We certainly don't "use up" the Holy Spirit, but in the daily grind of living we often let people and circumstances crowd out the Spirit's direction. This is why we need to "keep on being filled" with the Holy Spirit.

And by the way, this is not some mysterious spiritual process. We are filled with the Spirit as we consciously yield to Him and turn over every area of our lives to His control. As much as we might like to think we can do this once and be done with it, experience and the Word of God teach us that this isn't the case. Yielding control to the Spirit is a day-by-day, and often a moment-by-moment, necessity as we move through life.

I'm sure you've had the experience of coming to church and gathering with the saints of God to worship and praise Him and learn from His Word. The combination of the Word, the music, the praise, and the worship has filled you, and you leave church feeling like you can handle anything. But as the week goes on your filling is tapped by the trials of life and you soon find yourself in need of a refill. The goal of the Spirit's filling is to give you a fresh wind, a fresh fire, a new spiritual dynamic that enables you to live in accord with God's will.

We don't have to wonder what the Spirit's filling is like, because the Bible tells us in Ephesians 5:18. This verse begins, "Do not get drunk with wine" and tells us to be filled with the Spirit instead. We call it being under the influence of alcohol when the alcohol so possesses a person that it alters his personality and his actions. A drunk doesn't walk, talk, or act normal because the alcohol is now running the show and dictating the person's responses.

When you are filled with the Spirit, you come under His influence so God through the Spirit is now running the show and calling the shots in your life. Why can't some believers control their temper? Because they aren't drunk enough on the Holy Spirit. Why can't others overcome a wicked tongue, evil thoughts, or various addictions? Why are there so many powerless churches, constantly in conflict? Because they aren't Spirit-filled.

Now don't get me wrong. I'm not saying we can always just shed all of this stuff with one prayer, although I've seen the Spirit set people free instantly. What I'm saying is that we'll never get the victory in any area until the Holy Spirit is firmly in control.

Who Is Filling You?

If you are going to be filled with the Holy Spirit, you can't also be full of yourself, because the Spirit isn't going to take second place to your ego. What are the characteristics of people who are full of themselves? All they can think about and talk about is themselves, because they are all wrapped up in themselves.

Now turn that self-centeredness around and you have the

characteristics of Spirit-filled people. All they can talk and think about is God and what He is doing because He is continuously flowing through them in the power of the Spirit. I love the way Jesus pictured the Spirit's ministry as a constantly flowing stream of water (see John 7:37–39). The Holy Spirit does not want to minister to us in little spurts, but as a continuously flowing stream that is constantly refreshing and renewing us. In other words, the Spirit's filling is meant to be a way of life.

How to Get the Filling

If it is this important for us as the church to be filled with the Holy Spirit, the next logical question to ask is how we can get the filling that God commands us to have. God would not give us such a command without telling us how to fulfill it. The question of how to be filled with the Holy Spirit is answered in the three verses that follow Ephesians 5:18.

After giving the command to be filled, Paul went on to write, "Speaking to one another in psalms and hymns and spiritual songs, singing and making melody with your heart to the Lord; always giving thanks for all things in the name of our Lord Jesus Christ to God, even the Father; and be subject to one another in the fear of Christ" (vv. 19–21).

Let me summarize these verses. It is in the act and the attitude of worship that believers are filled with the Spirit. A church that wants to be a Spirit-filled church must be a worshiping church. A family that wants to be Spirit-filled must be a worshiping family. And if you want to be Spirit-filled as an individual believer, you must know what worship means and know how to worship.

Going back to our gas station analogy, worship is the fuel you get at the station when you come to be filled. Worship involves your relationship both with God and with other believers, which is why local church participation is essential for every believer. This is important because when the Holy Spirit came to indwell and fill the church in Acts 2, the church was gathered in collective worship. The believers were collectively filled with the Spirit again in Acts 4:23–31 as the church gathered to pray for boldness in their witness. The church gathered to worship and went out filled with the Spirit to serve Christ.

I'm not saying that you have to go to church in order to be filled with the Holy Spirit. You can go to church and not be a worshiper. You can go to church, sit back, and let the "professionals" on the stage do your worshiping for you.

But having said that, we shouldn't be surprised that the Spirit would grant His filling in the context of the church at worship. The Christian life was never intended to be a solo act. The Bible tells us to sing, not to and for ourselves alone, but "to one another" and to "the Lord." Our thanksgiving is to be directed to God the Father, and we are to be subject to one another, which means putting the interests of others ahead of our own and submitting to one another.

These things mentioned in Ephesians 5:19–21 are all forms of worship that put us in a dependent position in one way or another. They also require that we reach out to others for their benefit and blessing, not just our own. This is where the problem comes in, because too many believers don't want to be dependent worshipers. They want to be in control of their lives. They aren't that interested in blessing others, because they're too caught up in themselves and their needs. But we've already seen that being filled with the Spirit means yielding to His control. Therefore, no worship means no Spirit filling.

You see, God is not interested in filling and blessing you just for you. He wants to work through you. That's why the Bible brings the saints into the equation when it talks about the Holy Spirit's filling.

Why are so many of us Christians unwilling to become dependent worshipers who yield control of our lives to the Holy Spirit? Our problem is that we don't really believe John 15:5, which we quoted earlier. Jesus said, "Apart from Me you can do nothing." We may quote it, but in the practical sense we don't believe it. Because if we did, we would be falling on our faces before God, begging for His filling and His power. We would be praying, "Lord, I am desperate for You, because I cannot be the person You want me to be and do what You have asked me to do without the filling and empowering of Your Holy Spirit."

If we started praying that way as the collective body of Christ, we would see things happen that we haven't seen up to now. The main reason we think the events in the early church were so unusual and out of the ordinary is that we haven't really seen what God can do with a body of people who are filled with His Spirit and totally sold out to Him.

We may not be able to lift much weight, because the earth's strong gravitational pull is working against us. But if we were on the moon, we could be weightlifting champions because we have escaped the downward pull of our present environment. A lot of people in the body of Christ are being weighed down by a lot of problems and habits and addictions that they can't seem to shake. But if we were yielded to God and filled with the Holy Spirit, we would see burdens being lifted that some people thought were too heavy to be lifted. The Spirit's filling enables us to rise above the downward pull of circumstances and other things keeping us down.

So like a weight-lifter on the moon, what we need is to change our location. And we do that through worship as we place ourselves before God and confess our complete dependence on Him. When we do that, the Holy Spirit is free to pour in His filling. But doing this is going to require some adjustments on our part. Some of us need to start spending our time differently or hanging out with a different crowd. We're going to have to cultivate the joy and the discipline of being in God's presence, learning what it means to live in absolute trust and dependence on Him.

Now you understand why Jesus told the woman at the well that God the Father is seeking people who will worship Him "in spirit and truth" (John 4:23). These are the kind of people on whom God is eager to pour out His power and blessings through the ministry of the Holy Spirit. This is the kind of church God wants us to be, so we can know the Spirit's power for ourselves and turn this world upside down for Him, just like the early church did (see Acts 17:6).

THE MINISTRY OF THE CHURCH

6
THE WORSHIP OF THE CHURCH

If you received a nice-looking envelope in the mail that had your name handwritten on it and said, "Come join us: We're having a celebration," my guess is that you would open it right away. More than likely this invitation means that someone you care about is being honored for some special reason and other people you care about are getting together to celebrate the occasion.

People get together all the time to celebrate a friend or family member who is having a birthday or an anniversary, or who has earned a job promotion or some other honor. At these gatherings we expect to hear the invited guests speak well of the person being honored. The host or hostess may even ask several of the guests to tell what the honoree means to them or has done for them.

Celebrating special people on special occasions is in keeping with one of the primary definitions of the word *celebrate*, which is "to hold up for public acclaim." What we have just described is what the church is supposed to do when we come together as a body to worship our God and Head of the church. Corporate worship is the collective celebration of God for who He is, what He has done, and what we are trusting Him to do.

Although it's true that you can and should worship the Lord in your own private life, we will not be addressing the area of private worship in this chapter. My focus is on the church's worship, because something special happens when the family of God gathers in force to worship Him. God has written out the invitation to worship and sent it to us with our names on it. He invites His people to come into His presence in the great celebration that the Bible calls worship.

We have already seen that a celebration implies that there is someone to celebrate. This person could rightfully be called the celebrity, because this word simply means "a person being celebrated." A celebrity is the person in the spotlight, the one in the crowd to whom all eyes are turned.

You can see why Hollywood has cornered the market on the concept of celebrity today. When the stars come out for a special event in Hollywood, they arrive in limousines and walk down carpeted aisles with cameras and spotlights on them. There is no doubt in the mind of anyone present who is being honored—even if many celebrities' worthiness to be honored is questionable.

If the world can spotlight and honor its celebrities, how much more should the church be ready to honor and celebrate our God who is worthy of all praise. Worship says that God is the only truly worthy celebrity in the universe, so all of us who love Him ought to celebrate. The Bible says, "Praise is becoming [or fitting] to the upright" (Psalm 33:1).

WORSHIP LIFTS UP OUR GLORIOUS LORD

A phrase in the opening verses of Ephesians captures the basic content of the church's worship. There are a number of individual components to worship, but Ephesians 1:3 gives its foundation: "*Blessed* be the God and Father of our Lord Jesus Christ" (italics added).

Offering God Our Praise

The word *blessed* is from the Greek word eulogia, which means "to speak well of." You may recognize this as the source of the English word *eulogy*, which unfortunately we have come to associate only with funerals. But although the world may reserve its eulogies for the dead, the Bible calls the church to eulogize or speak well of our living God, and we do this when we gather for worship. "It is good to give thanks to the Lord and to sing praises to Your name, O Most High" (Psalm 92:1).

If it is your birthday, it is fitting for your friends and family to sing "Happy Birthday to You" and bless you on your special day. On your wedding anniversary, it is entirely appropriate for those around you to speak well of you and your spouse and tell you how much your example means to them. Just as events like these call for blessing and praise, God's person and work call for blessing and praise on the church's part.

You can see these elements of worship in a classic passage from Psalm 100, in which the psalmist calls us to worship: "Enter [God's] gates with thanksgiving and His courts with praise. Give thanks to Him, bless His name. For the Lord is good; His lovingkindness is everlasting and His faithfulness to all generations" (vv. 4–5).

Thanksgiving in the Bible is usually associated with worshiping God for what He has done, while blessing the Lord or praising Him often speaks about who He is. That's not a hard-and-fast rule, but it helps us see the various ways that we are to worship God.

In Ephesians 1, Paul gave us a great clue about what our worship should focus on. Paul rejoiced in the salvation God provided in Christ and also rejoiced that He did it "to the praise of the glory of His grace" (v. 6). Later Paul said that God designed it so that we who have trusted in Christ would be "to the praise of His glory" (v. 12).

Magnifying God's Glory

If God is focused on His glory—and we know that He is because the Bible teaches that God is jealous for His glory—then guess where our worship should be directed? Our job as worshipers in the church is to praise and exalt the glory of our great God.

To do that you and I have to be actively involved in worship. The church is not a theater where the spectators sit and watch the actors perform for their entertainment. God, not the church, is the audience in worship. I like the way David put in Psalm 34: "I will bless the Lord at all times; His praise shall continually be in my mouth" (v. 1). David connected praise and blessing, just as Paul did in the first chapter of Ephesians.

David continued in this psalm with an invitation to corporate worship: "O *magnify* the Lord with me, and let us exalt His name together" (v. 3, italics added). I want to look more closely at this concept of magnifying God, because it will help us understand what happens when we bless the Lord for being who He is and praise Him for what He has done and what He is going to do.

What happens when something is magnified? It is made to appear bigger in the eye of the person looking through the magnifying glass. You are going to say right away, "Tony, we can't make God any bigger than He already is."

That's true, because God already fills the universe and eternity. There is no lack in God that requires us to magnify Him so He will look big. Instead, the key is what I said above, that when we magnify something it looks bigger *to us*. The idea of magnifying the Lord is that when you focus your praise lens on Him, you see Him for the great and awesome God that He really is, and suddenly God looks bigger than your problems or your circumstances—which is the way things are supposed to look to believers. And when the church gathers to praise and magnify the Lord as a body, all of the believers have the opportunity to see Him and see life in true perspective.

Your situation may have God looking pretty small in your life right now. If so, you're not alone in feeling that way. David and the other writers of the Psalms often cried out to God, "Where are You, and why aren't You coming to my aid?" (see Psalm 22:1). The writer of Psalm 73 was in almost total despair because it seemed that the wicked were prospering while he suffered for being righteous (vv. 1–16). But in verse 17 something happened. "I came into the sanctuary of God," the writer said, and his entire perspective changed (read vv. 17–28). All of a sudden, God looked very big and the wicked looked very small.

That's the power worship has to change us when we go together into God's presence in His house. Have you ever gone to church when God seemed small and distant, and left with Him seeming big and close because you were drawn closer to Him in worship? That's what happens when we magnify the Lord and bless His name together.

The Power of Collective Praise

I said we wouldn't address the issue of private worship, but I need to stop and deal with a very common objection that comes up when we talk about the necessity and importance of worshiping the Lord with other saints in the church. Someone will say, "I don't need to go to church to worship God. I can sing hymns and praise God and worship Him by myself at home, out on the lake, or in the woods."

It's true that any believer can worship God anywhere. But God never meant that to be a substitute for the church's collective worship. That's why the Bible exhorts us not to forsake assembling ourselves together (see Hebrews 10:25). The fact is that a lot of good things happen when the church gathers that are missing in private worship.

Two of those good things are found in the two verses immediately preceding Hebrews 10:25. "Let us hold fast the confession of our hope without wavering," and, "Let us consider how to stimulate one another to love and good deeds" (vv. 23–24). You will hold fast to your confession in Christ a lot better when you have other Christians around you holding up your hands in encouragement and calling you to accountability. Also, it's pretty hard to stimulate other believers to love and good deeds when you're not with them. And since God also promises to meet with His people (see Matthew 18:20), there is a definite sense in which the presence of God is among His people in a special way when we join together to worship Him.

We said earlier that worship demands our participation, not our spectatorship. If you want to see God magnified and lifted up, then you need to lift up your heart and voice to praise Him. When I preach a microphone amplifies, or magnifies, my ordinary voice so that everyone in the sanctuary can hear it. When we open our mouths to bless and praise the Lord, the Holy Spirit amplifies our worship and God is magnified in our midst. Try that at the lake by yourself; it's not the same.

Showing God Off

We are told in Psalm 29:2, "Ascribe to the Lord the glory due to His name; worship the Lord in holy array." To ascribe glory to the Lord means to show Him off, to put Him on display so everyone can see how glorious and wonderful He is. Remember the definition of *celebrate,* which is "to hold up for public acclaim." Glorifying the Lord means that you want His name to become greater and greater.

Whenever I read this verse, I think of the sports world. Sports fans have no problem ascribing glory to their heroes, and doing so in public with loud voices and shouting—even sometimes when their heroes aren't doing anything that's worthy of such acclaim. So why should the church be reluctant to loudly declare God's praises? He is worthy to be blessed!

In writing to the Ephesians, Paul got so excited about God and His glory that he forgot to use good grammar. The first twelve verses of Ephesians 1 are one long, run-on sentence in the original Greek text. When you get your praise on, you don't worry about grammar because you are so passionate to make the point that God is worthy to be praised.

One reason we're not seeing more of God's glory in the church is that we're not praising Him more. Little praise in the church equals a little view of God rather than a magnified view of Him. A lot of praise equals a lot of God, because God is "enthroned upon" or "inhabits" the praises of His people (Psalm 22:3). He loves it when His people gather in the congregation to worship Him.

The Bible calls us to give God the glory that is due Him. God's glory is different from human glory because it is intrinsic rather than ascribed. We could illustrate ascribed glory by using police officers or judges as an example. We give such people "glory" or honor by virtue of their position and the uniform they wear to symbolize that position. A police officer's glory is tied to the uniform and badge, while we recognize and acknowledge a judge who is wearing a black robe.

When police officers or judges take off the symbols of their authority, they are just like everybody else. That doesn't mean we don't need to respect them, but neither they nor any other human being has "built-in" glory that is theirs just because of who they are.

But God has intrinsic glory that is an essential part of His person. God is glorious because His nature is filled with glory. "May the whole earth be filled with His glory" the psalmist declared (Psalm 72:19). God calls His church together to recognize who He is, worship Him, and magnify His glory. We go to the house of the Lord to meet with the Lord of the house. His name is due all the glory, and the church has been given the glorious task of declaring God's glory to the world.

WORSHIP LIFTS US TO A HIGHER PLACE

Another reason the church gathers for worship is that when we lift the Lord up, He lifts us up to a higher place that only those who know and worship Him can reach. This higher place is described in Ephesians 1:3, which we need to look at again, this time adding the second phrase: "Blessed be the God and Father of our Lord Jesus Christ, who has blessed us with every spiritual blessing in the heavenly places in Christ."

Reaching the Heavenly Places

We bless the Lord who has already blessed us with every spiritual resource we will ever need to live the way He wants us to live and do what He wants us to do. But notice where these blessings are located. They are in "the heavenly places," which refers to the spiritual realm where the capital of the universe is located and where God rules. That's where you and I need to go for our blessings, and worship takes us there.

One of the fundamental principles of Scripture, which we have talked about before, is that everything in the physical realm is initiated in or influenced by the spiritual realm. Most of our problems, struggles, and needs are in the physical realm, but if we never access the heavenly places where our Lord and our spiritual blessings are located, then our solutions will be limited to the physical level, which is always temporary. If you want to fix something that's wrong in the physical realm, but affected by the spiritual realm, you have to go to the spiritual realm for your solution.

You see, a bad attitude may manifest itself in bad language and bad actions, but those are the fruit and not the root of the problem. A bad attitude is a spiritual problem. If there's conflict in your home or at work, there is a spiritual problem at its root. But if you don't know how to bless the Lord so you can go to the heavenly places, then you won't get to the root of the need.

This is why God's people ought to come to church to encounter Him in authentic worship, not to watch what's happening or just gather more information about God. There's a world of difference between coming to church to meet your friends or hear a sermon and coming to church to meet God. As a pastor I can preach a sermon that maybe isn't one of my best or doesn't seem to connect with the hearers, and yet some people in the congregation can still leave church having heard from the Lord because they came to meet Him and blessed Him with all of their hearts and souls.

Seeing God Face-to-Face

If you've ever been on a blind date, you know such events are risky business. You don't know what you're getting yourself into when a friend wants to fix you up with someone you haven't met. Your friend can describe your prospective date in all kinds of glowing terms and make the person sound wonderful, but all of that information isn't enough to satisfy you. Why? Because you want to see the other person for yourself. You want to have a face-to-face encounter. After all of Job's trials were over and he had an encounter with God, he said, "I have heard of You by the hearing of the ear; but now my eye sees You" (Job 42:5). And he was a chastened and changed person.

You don't want to come to church like you're going on a blind date. The pastor can give you good information about God and make Him sound glorious, but information is not enough. If you want to know God and experience Him in your worship, you need to see Him face-to-face. That is what happens when you get your praise on and God transports you to heavenly places. That's where you want to be, because your blessings are located there, not on earth.

A lot of Christians don't ever get to heavenly places because they don't know how to worship. In the opening chapters of the book of Revelation, the risen Lord Jesus is moving among the golden lampstands that represent the church. He is moving among His people, and He has a message that He wants the angel, or the pastor, of each church to deliver to the people.

But the Lord also knows that not everyone in the church is listening to Him or seeking Him, which is why He ends each message of Revelation 2–3 with these words: "He who has an ear, let him hear what the Spirit says to the churches" (see Revelation 2:7 as an example). God is speaking to the whole church, but only those who are tuned to God in worship will respond to the message.

Worship transforms you to a higher place, where the Holy Spirit moves and works. But this is not just an individual thing with you and Jesus and no one else. Paul said the church is "being fitted together, [and] is growing into a holy temple in the Lord, in whom you also are being built together into a dwelling of God in the Spirit" (Ephesians 2:21–22). God wants us to understand that we are part of something bigger than our own small world.

When the people of God join in His praise, worship, and adoration, His Spirit is free to work in mighty ways. He lifts us to another kingdom, where there is peace, joy, power, goodness, grace, and mercy. This is a totally different world than any you have ever known before, and it can be accessed as you bless the Lord in community with the saints.

WORSHIP SHOULD BE A PRIORITY

Knowing this ought to make worship a priority for all of us, something we do first instead of last. The psalmist who wrote Psalm 73 in despair over the seeming prosperity of the wicked was about ready to give up. Things didn't change for him until he made his way to God's sanctuary to enter His presence. Then his perspective on earth changed because he saw the spiritual reality behind the physical world around him.

The church experienced the same thing in Acts 4 when Peter and John had been arrested for preaching Christ. They were released with threats, but the church members came together and lifted up their voices to God in praise and supplication (see Acts 4:23–30). When they finished their prayer the Bible says, "The place where they had gathered together was shaken, and they were all filled with the Holy Spirit and began to speak the word of God with boldness" (v. 31). The church was lifted to heavenly places and got the real story on the situation, which caused them to preach Christ rather than fear the authorities.

How hungry are you to encounter God in worship and be transported to heavenly places? The degree of your hunger will determine the degree of your satisfaction. When a baby is hungry, a pacifier won't do. But a baby who isn't hungry is content to suck on a pacifier.

I fear that too many Christians come to church wanting to be pacified instead of bringing with them a gnawing hunger to seek and worship God that demands to be met. As long as the choir can stick a little song in their mouths to suck on, they're fine. As long as the pastor sticks a little sermon in their mouths to pacify them, they're fine.

But what happens when a baby is really hungry? He will turn the place into chaos to get his hunger satisfied. A baby doesn't care about what other people think or who might be upset with him if he has a hunger that only real food can satisfy.

When you go to church, you ought to go hungry to worship God and enter the heavenly realm. One reason God allows things to go wrong during the week is to make you hungry for Him. He'll make you dependent to drive you to His house where you can meet Him. When you are in desperate need of God, then you are ready to worship Him because you know you have a hunger and a need that He alone can satisfy.

There's a great story in Exodus 17:8–16 of Israel's war with the Amalekites. You may remember that Moses went up on a mountain and lifted his hands over the battlefield while Joshua and the army fought below. As long as Moses' hands stayed up, Israel prevailed. But Moses grew tired and his hands fell, and the Amalekites began to win. So Aaron and Hur sat Moses down on a rock and held up his hands, and Israel won a great victory. As long as Moses' hands were pointed toward heaven, God changed things on earth.

Sometimes you come to church too tired in your spirit to worship and to access the heavenly realm. Sometimes you come too beaten down to worship, and your hands drop to your side. That's when you need the other members of the body of Christ to come alongside you and lift your hands so that you are strengthened and lifted to the realm of heaven.

You say, "But you don't know what's happening on earth." No, you don't know what God can do from heaven when you enter the heavenly realm through worship and praise of Him.

WORSHIP CONNECTS US
WITH GOD'S POWER

Worship that lifts the name of the Lord and lifts you to a higher realm also puts you in connection with God's power. I love the way Paul linked worship with power in his prayer of Ephesians 3:

> I bow my knees before the Father, from whom every family in heaven and on earth derives its name, that He would grant you, according to the riches of His glory, to be strengthened with power through His Spirit in the inner man, so that Christ may dwell in your hearts through faith; and that you, being rooted and grounded in love, may be able to comprehend with all the saints what is the breadth and length and height and depth, and to know the love of Christ which surpasses knowledge, that you may be filled up to all the fullness of God. (vv. 14–19)

Most of the time when we quote this passage, we quote it as a personal and private promise of God's power. But that's not what the text says. This is plural, written to the church as Christ's body when we gather to worship Him. Verses 20–21 also make this very clear. "Now to Him who is able to do far more abundantly beyond all that we ask or think, according to the power that works within us, to Him be the glory in the church and in Christ Jesus to all generations forever and ever. Amen."

Experiencing God's Power Together

There is power in our worship, because when the saints of God bless His name together He is able to do abundant things, far beyond anything we can imagine. The world long ago discovered the power that is available to change things when a lot of folk get together to do what one person alone can't do.

This is the principle behind the labor unions that changed the face of the American workplace. Individually, the workers had very little power to bring about change. But when they united, they had a voice and a presence that their bosses had to reckon with.

I don't think we read passages like Ephesians 3 often enough in church or think about them long enough. The Bible says that God wants to do far more for us than we could ever imagine, if He can only find enough worshipers. There is power in worship because God honors and blesses the worship of His people when we bless His name and hold Him up to public acclaim. But this only happens when "all the saints" are in the house.

I'm afraid that our selfish and individualistic age has infiltrated the mind-set of God's people. Too many people continue to view faith as a private matter between them and God, and the church seems to be an extra that they can take or leave. But God doesn't pour out His choicest blessings on selfish children who refuse to become an active part of His body. A child in a large family who suddenly decides that he or she is the only one who counts is going to cause a lot of problems.

It's true that loving parents are still going to feed and clothe a selfish, uncooperative child, but they are hardly going to be motivated to give in to that child's demands and "bless" him or her with the best they have to give. Why should we expect God to do that for us when we're problem children in His family? Too many believers aren't seeing the power of God because they don't understand that Christianity has to do with all of the saints. God designed us to be part of a local body of believers, and He is going to work through that assembly to bless and chastise and grow us up.

And when the family of God worships and prays together, then we can get ready to see something happen. Then we will see God doing "far more abundantly beyond all that we ask or think." It's the difference between one person standing in the darkness with a little candle, and a whole group of people lighting the candles of the people next to them. Many churches have a service like this at Christmas or some other special time when they give everyone candles and then turn out the lights in the sanctuary. As each candle is lit, the light grows. It's a powerful reminder of why we need the body of Christ.

Experiencing God's Blessings Together

I recently came across an amazing passage in Zechariah 14:17. The prophet was speaking of Christ's millennial kingdom when He will rule over all the earth from His throne in Jerusalem: "And it will be that whichever of the families of the earth does not go up to Jerusalem to worship the King, the Lord of hosts, there will be no rain on them."

Rain is symbolic of God's blessings. God says that people who don't have time to worship Him will not experience His blessings. If His glory isn't important enough for people to acknowledge through worship at His house, then those people's needs will be answered not with showers of blessing, but with a few sprinkles here and there.

Many Christians are satisfied with a few raindrops from God—until trouble hits. Then they want to do a rain dance and ask God to open the windows of heaven and pour down help on them. But God says, "I am looking at your worship to determine your rain."

Power strips are a great invention because they make more electricity available to you from the same outlet. Now instead of one plug you can plug six or even eight plugs into the power source. That's a picture of the way God wants the church to function. It's one thing to pray by yourself and for yourself, and there's nothing wrong with that. But when the people of God join our prayers in the body, we create a vehicle through which God can work in greater power.

As you move through your week, you are operating in enemy territory. You are immersed in a world that Satan owns and controls and through which he is determined to knock you down and defeat you. But when you come to church, you get what is called in sports the home court or home field advantage. Now you're in God's house with His team. And when you have the rest of the team holding you up and glorifying God with you, you have an advantage that you can take back into the world. You can bring your losses and discouragements to church and turn them into victories, because on the home court of the church, things are going to be different.

Don't just go to church to hear what the pastor has to say, or listen to what the choir is going to sing. Go to see what God has to say through the choir and through the pastor as they share the Word. Go to worship God in fellowship with all the saints, and then watch Him open the windows of heaven and rain His goodness on His people.

7

THE FELLOWSHIP OF THE CHURCH

The story is told of a man in a small town whose loved one died without having any funeral arrangements made. When the man discovered that the deceased did not have a burial plot, he went to the head of the local parish seeking permission to bury his loved one in the parish's fenced-in graveyard. But he was told, "I'm sorry, but this graveyard is reserved for members of our church. Besides, there isn't room for an extra grave inside the fence."

The man went away disappointed, but the next day he got word that a grave had been dug inside the fence for his family member. He went to the head of the parish and said, "I don't understand. We're not members here, and you said there wasn't any room anyway. How did we get a place inside the fence?"

The parish official said, "I thought about it last night, and I simply moved the fence."

What that parish official did for a person in need is what God has done for the human race. He has "moved the fence" by reaching out to us in grace so that people who were outside the fence can come inside through faith in Jesus Christ. And anyone who is inside the fence not only becomes a child of God, but is also related to the rest of God's children because the Bible says, "We are members of one another" (Ephesians 4:25). Believers are knit together in a bond of family fellowship that is critical to the church's function. None of us is in this thing alone.

THE REALITY OF OUR FELLOWSHIP

The church's fellowship is a relational reality that reflects the relational nature of God. God has never known what it is like to be alone, because one of the foundational truths of our faith is that God is a triune being, eternally existing as Father, Son, and Holy Spirit in a perfect fellowship of distinct Persons who share the same essence. Jesus said at one point in His earthly ministry, "He who sent Me is with Me; He has not left Me alone, for I always do the things that are pleasing to Him" (John 8:29).

So we ought not be surprised that relationships are very important to God. The only thing that God said was not good about His creation was that Adam was "alone" (Genesis 2:18). The first relational statement made about the human race was that God did not design us to function as isolated units. When Jesus chose His twelve disciples, Mark noted that one of Jesus' purposes was "so that they would be with Him" (Mark 3:14).

God is a relational being who not only enjoys fellowship within the Godhead, but also seeks to have fellowship with His creatures. The ultimate expression of God's desire for fellowship with human beings is the church, a body of people that God has called out from the world to be His children.

Fellowship is so important to the church's proper functioning that it stands as one of the foundational activities we are to engage in, along with discipleship, worship, proclamation, and evangelism. The Greek term for the church's fellowship is *koinonia*, which basically means "to share" or "hold in common." What we hold in common as the church, the thing that brings us together from a myriad of cultures and races and backgrounds, is our faith in Jesus Christ.

So let me give you a more formal definition of Christian fellowship or *koinonia*. It is the mutual sharing of the life of Christ among believers. The church is a family affair, a group of people coming together so all can partake of our mutual faith in Christ.

It needs to be said right away that when we talk about fellowship, we are not talking about having punch and cookies in the church's fellowship hall. There's nothing wrong with that, but fellowship is much more substantial. Many Christians in our culture would be shocked to learn that it's possible to have biblical fellowship without food or drink.

Fellowship in the Truth

The Bible has a lot to say about the church's fellowship, and no book is more important on this subject than 1 John. In fact, John made this statement about his purpose in writing this letter to the church: "What we have seen and heard we proclaim to you also, so that you too may have fellowship *[koinonia]* with us; and indeed our fellowship is with the Father, and with His Son Jesus Christ" (1:3).

The rest of 1 John makes it abundantly clear that John's concern was not just that believers enjoy some good times together. He wanted to make sure that the church's coming together was anchored in the truth about who Jesus Christ is and what He did for us on the cross. A group of people drinking together at a bar during "happy hour" may be enjoying one another's company, but their gathering is not anchored in the truth, and their purpose is not to further the truth and build each other up in the truth.

One interesting clue to the important place that fellowship holds in the body of Christ is found in Galatians 2:9. Paul said that when the church in Jerusalem recognized that God was working through him and Barnabas, then "James and Cephas and John, who were reputed to be pillars, gave to me and Barnabas the right hand of fellowship." That is, these leaders signaled that they were one in unity and purpose with Paul and Barnabas, and members of the same body. The word *fellowship* here is almost a synonym for the church.

We drew from this idea when we named our church in Dallas. We could have called it Oak Cliff Bible Church, and that would have been accurate. But we wanted to emphasize one of the key experiences that God has given to His people, so we decided to call our church the Oak Cliff Bible Fellowship.

What we wanted to say with this name is that the church is more than a school for spiritual instruction, a theater for spiritual performance, or an organization carrying out spiritual programs. The church is a living entity made up of people who have been called by God to live in relationship with Him and with each other.

The Two Dimensions of Fellowship

You see, biblical fellowship has two dimensions, the vertical and the horizontal. John said, "Our fellowship is with the Father, and with His Son Jesus Christ." This is the vertical aspect of fellowship, while the horizontal concerns our relationship with one another. Both aspects are crucial.

For instance, if there is no vertical fellowship with God, then whatever we do on earth is without real meaning because it is not based on truth. John wrote, "If we say that we have fellowship with [God] and yet walk in the darkness, we lie and do not practice the truth" (1 John 1:6).

If we have horizontal fellowship but no vertical fellowship, then we are not holding to a common faith, which is the very basis of biblical fellowship. But if we have vertical fellowship without horizontal fellowship, then the thing we're holding in common is not benefiting anybody but us. If God only had one spiritual child, he or she wouldn't have to worry about fellowship on earth. But God's family is full of children from every corner of the world.

In Ephesians 2:11–22, Paul talked about how Jews and Gentiles had been brought together in Christ. Here were two groups of people who would normally have little if anything to do with each other. And yet, as believers in Christ, they were now reconciled "in one body" and had become "fellow citizens with the saints" and part of "God's household" (vv. 16, 19). This fellowship superseded and canceled out all of the old hostilities between Jews and Gentiles and broke down the wall of religion and culture separating them.

If you go to Israel today you won't find a lot of churches. But in those that exist you will find Jews and Arabs worshiping together because they have been made a part of God's household in Christ. These people have nothing else in common in terms of their background and heritage, but they have come together around the faith in Christ that they hold in common.

Everyone is welcome in Christ regardless of background, class, or race. That's why you can't bring the world's mess of prejudice and exclusiveness into the church. It's not that we deny who we are, but we subjugate these issues to the greater cause of the gospel. That's why there can be no real movement of the Spirit of God when there is no authentic fellowship among His people. Too many churches are like Frankenstein's monster as it lay on the table in the laboratory—anatomically correct, structurally accurate, but with no real life because there is no *koinonia*.

How Fellowship Reveals the Unseen

Why is fellowship so important to the church? Why does God place us in an environment of *koinonia*? One reason is that He wants to make the invisible visible through you and me. Later in his first epistle, John made an important statement: "Beloved, if God so loved us, we also ought to love one another. No one has seen God at any time; if we love one another, God abides in us, and His love is perfected in us" (1 John 4:11–12).

You can't see God, who is invisible. But His presence in your life becomes real as you love your brothers and sisters in Christ's body. God will make Himself at home in your life through the Holy Spirit, and His presence will become visibly real to you—not through your physical eyes, but in terms of your spiritual experience. He will give you the vertical reality you're looking for as you make the horizontal connection with other believers.

A lot of Christians pray, "Lord, draw me close to You" while they are estranged from other believers. God's response is "I am waiting for you to draw close to someone else." If God cannot make you a vehicle to express His love, He won't make you a container to receive His love.

We've dealt before with the argument some people make that they don't have to be part of the church to get saved. That's right, you don't have to be a member of a church to go to heaven. But if you want to see some of heaven down here on earth, you had better join yourself to a local body of Christ and become part of the fellowship. The reason some people aren't seeing the invisible God manifested in their lives is because they are not practicing *koinonia*.

How Fellowship Validates Our Faith

Our participation in the body also validates the reality of our relationship with God. That's what 1 John 4:11–12 is saying. You cannot have intimate fellowship with God if He cannot have intimate fellowship through you to somebody else. Someone has said that the only Jesus some people will see is the Jesus they see in us. That's true not only for lost people, but it's true in the church as well. God becomes real to us, and to others, when He works through us to touch their lives.

So if your life is a spiritual cul-de-sac, with no outlet, instead of a conduit, you are cutting off a large portion of God's blessing to and through you. If you don't have time to minister to somebody else, God says He doesn't have time to minister to you. God is so big that we cannot possibly see or comprehend even a small portion of the totality of His being. But the quality of our fellowship gives us a valve or gauge that indicates whether God is working within us.

My old elementary school was heated by a huge boiler down in the boiler room. When I asked the janitor how it worked, he explained that the big tank heated the water, which turned to steam and was sent up to the radiators in the classrooms. When I asked him how he knew when there was enough water in the tank, he showed me a little tube on top of the boiler.

"I can't look inside the boiler, because it's too hot," he said. "So if I want to know how much water is in the tank, I look at the water level in this tube."

We can't look inside the nature of God. He's too big to fathom. But through our fellowship with one another, He has given us an indicator of His presence within us. If your fellowship is low, then your relationship with the "boiler" is low. God takes our fellowship very seriously because He has made us to be members of one another.

Certainly our fellowship as believers involves prayer, study of the Word, sharing of needs and victories, and all of the other ways that believers connect with each other. But true *koinonia* also goes beyond these things.

John described that something more for us: "We know love by this, that He laid down His life for us; and we ought to lay down our lives for the brethren. But whoever has the world's goods, and sees his brother in need and closes his heart against him, how does the love of God abide in him? Little children, let us not love with word or with tongue, but in deed and truth" (1 John 3:16–18). In other words, love involves doing, not just saying. It is visible, not just verbal. Fellowship involves touching the life of somebody else in a way that meets the need and makes a real difference.

THE POWER OF OUR FELLOWSHIP

I hope you realize by now that there is power in fellowship. The Holy Spirit works uniquely when believers are in dynamic relationship with God and with one another. The early church's experience is a classic example of this power.

The Power of a Shared Commitment

As those first disciples waited for the coming of the Spirit that Jesus had promised, the Bible says, "These all with one mind were continually devoting themselves to prayer" (Acts 1:14). Then on the day of Pentecost "they were all together in one place" (Acts 2:1) when the Spirit came with the sound of a rushing wind.

And in the days following Pentecost as the church ministered and grew, the believers faithfully devoted themselves to fellowship along with the teaching of the Word, sharing the Lord's Supper, and prayer (see Acts 2:42). Verse 44 also makes a very insightful statement: "All those who had believed were together and had all things in common," which is another form of the word *koinonia*.

Because these Christians practiced true fellowship, they had no problem sharing their possessions with anyone who was in need (see v. 45; Barnabas is the great example of this generosity, as we'll see later). The church was also of "one mind," and the believers "were taking their meals together with gladness and sincerity of heart" (v. 46). No wonder Acts 2 concludes, "And the Lord was adding to their number day by day those who were being saved" (v. 47). This church had power with God and power with people.

Do you get the point? The Holy Spirit showed up when these believers got together in purposeful fellowship. This was more than just meeting for a meal or to hang out with each other. The power of God was so obvious in their presence that Acts 2:43 says, "Everyone kept feeling a sense of awe; and many wonders and signs were taking place through the apostles."

True *koinonia* not only frees God up to do more for us, but it also frees God up through His Holy Spirit to do more among us. When the church is united in spirit and purpose, we will see God do things among us and through us that we are not likely to see happen apart from that dynamic relationship of believers. We saw that Ephesians 5:18 commands us to be filled with the Holy Spirit and then sets that filling in the context of our ministry to one another in the body of Christ. The church in the books of Acts was together when they were filled with the Spirit. The Spirit invaded the whole environment.

I like to compare the church's fellowship to logs in a fireplace. It's hard to burn a single log, because it takes a lot to get it lighted and keep it burning, and it doesn't provide much warmth or last very long anyway. But a stack of logs burns for a long time and draws people to the warmth and the light. This is a picture of the church that is practicing biblical fellowship. The world may not marvel at the church's routines, but when we are demonstrating the reality and power of God's presence among us people will be drawn to the flame—to watch us burn, if nothing else.

The Power of Generosity

There is one especially powerful example of the church's *koinonia* at the end of Acts 4 and the beginning of Acts 5. These verses are a study in contrasts between the church at large and Barnabas in particular, and a couple named Ananias and Sapphira.

Acts 4:32 tells us, "The congregation of those who believed were of one heart and soul; and not one of them claimed that anything belonging to him was his own, but all things were common property to them." The believers in Jerusalem were so closely knit together in heart, so drawn together as members of one another, that they didn't even bother to distinguish one person's possessions from another's.

The result was "There was not a needy person among them" (v. 34). These Christians were all on the same page when it came to meeting needs in the congregation. They were all pulling in the same direction. When you find a church full of people who are ready to open their homes, their refrigerators, and their wallets to others who are in need, that's one strong indication that you have located a church with dynamic, Spirit-inspired fellowship.

Don't misunderstand what the Bible is saying here. It doesn't say that the believers didn't have any belongings of their own. We are not talking about communism. It says that they didn't claim their possessions in the sense of selfishly hoarding them and saying to the apostles,

"No way. This is my stuff. You can't touch it." They understood that everything they had belonged to God anyway and was just on loan to them. This is a lesson we need to learn, because we're in the same position. Everything you can hold in your hands or point to as belonging to you will either leave you someday, or you will leave it.

Let's admit that this is a hard lesson to learn, and one we need to be constantly reminded of. What better place to learn and practice this lesson than in the fellowship of believers? That's what was happening in the early church at Jerusalem. No one set out to teach a lesson on stewardship. This generosity came out of the overflow of the believers' fellowship. Selfish Christians want to be ministered to, but they aren't interested in ministering to others. But that's not the case with the congregation of Acts 4.

Before we consider Barnabas, notice the impact of the church's fellowship: "And with great power the apostles were giving testimony to the resurrection of the Lord Jesus, and abundant grace was upon them all" (Acts 4:33). The power of God was greatly evident among them, and His abundant grace rested upon them. These people got to see God do things that were far beyond church business as usual. And they experienced grace that was, as the hymn says, greater than all their needs. God's power and grace show up when the church is fellowshiping according to His standards.

Barnabas stepped out of this context and distinguished himself by an extraordinary act of generosity. He sold a piece of land he owned, then "brought the money and laid it at the apostles' feet" (Acts 4:37). That's the end of his part, because nothing else needed to be said. Barnabas gave it all.

But then we come to Ananias and Sapphira (see Acts 5:1–11), who tried to enjoy God's full blessing while holding out on Him and their fellow believers in need. You can read the story of how they lied to the Holy Spirit and paid for their sin with their lives. Ananias and Sapphira were struck dead because they lied to God, and because of the damage that their lie did. These two were pretending to minister to their fellow Christians who were hurting, but by their actions they hurt the body of Christ.

Now let me tell you something. According to 1 Corinthians 3:17, "If any man destroys the temple of God, God will destroy him." God is so zealous for His body, the church, that He brings judgment on those who tamper with it. God is so committed to His family that when you mess with it, He will take you out. The sobering story of Ananias and Sapphira takes place in the setting of the church's fellowship. This is serious stuff.

THE CONTEXT OF OUR FELLOWSHIP

The Bible makes it clear that the church's fellowship occurs in the context of our assembling together. There are three important admonitions to the church in Hebrews 10, which the writer sets in this context: "Since we have a great priest over the house of God" (v. 21). In other words, he is speaking to the collective church as the household or family of God. In other words, we do not assemble just to hear good sermons, but also to form meaningful relationships that build one another up in the faith.

Drawing Back

Since we have Jesus Christ ministering as our great high priest, we need to do three things. First, "Let us draw near" together before Him in worship (Hebrews 10:22), "Let us hold fast" to our common faith (v. 23), and "Let us consider how to stimulate one another to love and good deeds, not forsaking our own assembling together" (vv. 24–25). This is a powerful formula for a church that wants to establish a context or environment in which dynamic, biblical fellowship can flourish.

We could summarize these commands by saying, "Let us not stay at home and draw back from one another in isolation, but let us draw near to God and to one another so we can hang in there together and be strong." Hebrews 10:25 says it is "the habit of some" to forsake the assembly. This is the Easter and Christmas crowd, the people who have little experience of the life and power of God because they have forsaken the family.

Notice what happens when the church is united in true fellowship. We not only stimulate each other to love and good works, but we encourage each other (see Hebrews 3:13; 10:25b). If the devil's favorite weapon is discouragement, then we had better be encouraging one another. If you want to become discouraged and tempted to give up, just try going it alone day after day and week after week. This is why it is crucial that churches develop mechanisms to teach people on an intimate individual level. Whether it be through home groups, ministry groups, or Sunday school classes, every church must make sure it facilitates biblical fellowship for every member of the body.

My daughter Priscilla was a cheerleader in high school. The amazing thing is that she and the cheerleaders often cheered the most when the team was behind. Why? Because it's when you're behind that you need encouragement the most. When you're on top of things, you don't feel the need for encouragement. But when your heart is broken and the load is heavy, you need to have somebody cheering for you and encouraging you in the Lord.

I don't know about you, but sometimes I go to church weighed down with burdens. Now I'm the pastor and I get paid to lift other people up, but I need to be lifted and encouraged too, because I experience many of the same things that burden the people in our church. We need each other, because together we can form a strong bond to support each other.

The church's fellowship reminds me of a wicker chair. One or two strands of a wicker chair could not hold a person's weight by themselves, but when enough strands are woven together the chair can easily bear a person's weight. It's the sum total of the wicker strands joined in "fellowship" that makes the chair work. No pastor can bear the weight of a congregation alone without collapsing. That's why all of us have to work hard at developing *koinonia*.

Paul wrote, "Blessed be the God and Father of our Lord Jesus Christ, the Father of mercies and God of all comfort, who comforts us in all our affliction so that we will be able to comfort those who are in any affliction with the comfort with which we ourselves are comforted by God" (2 Corinthians 1:3–4). As God meets us in our need for comfort or encouragement, He also enables us and even expects us to meet someone else's need.

You see, too many people look at the service of fellowship as an irritation or an interruption instead of an opportunity to serve others. But God meets our needs so that we can be ready when it's our turn to comfort someone else. You know a church is growing and making progress when in addition to its "official" ministries of helping the sick and lonely and hurting, individual believers are being led by the Holy Spirit to reach out to others in unofficial ways.

Whenever the Spirit brings someone to mind and tugs on your heart to help that person, He is saying, "It's your turn to serve." That's why when we gather as the church, it's not just to pray and sing and hear the Word, but to allow the Holy Spirit opportunities to sensitize our hearts toward others and show us how we can serve the body.

A mother whose little girl was lost in a big field of tall grass was frantically trying to find her. The mother ran wildly and haphazardly around the field, but she realized she wasn't getting anywhere and called for help. Soon there was a large group of people running around in the field individually, but they still couldn't find the girl. Finally, someone suggested that they all join hands and walk across the field together in one great sweep. They soon found the child. That's how fellowship is designed to work.

A Special Access Road

I was on my way downtown in Dallas one day recently and got stuck in heavy traffic. That was frustrating enough, but the mess was even harder to endure because when I looked to my left, I saw a whole line of cars flying past me at full speed. The reason is that they were in what is called the HOV or "High Occupancy Vehicle" lane, a lane specially constructed for cars with two or more people in them. I was stuck in traffic and could not enjoy the "fellowship" of the HOV lane drivers because I was alone in my car that day. The HOV program is designed not only to facilitate traffic, but to discourage drivers from doing their own little independent driving thing and encourage people to start traveling in groups.

So there I was, a lone driver going nowhere with a bunch of other lone drivers going nowhere, while the "fellowshipers" in the special lane were sailing along to their destination. If you are willing to travel in fellowship, there's a special access lane made just for you. God has some blessings ready for you that the "loners" don't get to experience. And by the way, you can't sneak in on the blessings without practicing *koinonia*, because if you try to get in the special access lane while driving by yourself, there is a police officer there to flag you down and give you a ticket. You can't bluff your way on this one.

As long as you and I decide that we are happy being independent, self-centered Christians, God is going to cause us to get bogged down somewhere along the line until we open our eyes and realize that *koinonia* is the way to go. We'll get there faster when we do things God's way. So which way are you going to travel to heaven? God has a special access lane for you—access in prayer, access in power, access in privileges, access in blessing—when He sees that you are willing to travel with somebody else.

8

THE PROCLAMATION OF THE CHURCH

When my granddaughter Kariss comes to stay at our house, she usually wants doughnuts for breakfast. I am not supposed to buy any doughnuts for myself, but I can hardly say no when Kariss looks at me and says, "Poppy, I want to get some doughnuts." So like a good grandfather, I take her up the street to the doughnut shop.

Kariss usually wants glazed doughnuts, but while we're there I figure I might as well show her some other kinds she should consider. She usually goes for my choices, so by the time we get home there are more doughnuts in the box than she can eat by herself. We have taught her not to waste food, so when Kariss says, "Poppy, I can't eat all of these—will you help me?" I feel obligated to respond as a good grandfather. Not wanting to contradict the lesson that we have been teaching her, I assist my granddaughter with the doughnuts. That way I can eat doughnuts, but say I didn't buy any for myself!

This doesn't happen very often, which is good because there is one major problem with doughnuts as a meal. They are succulent, but insignificant when it comes to any real nutritional value. They taste sweet and bring momentary pleasure, but they don't leave anything of lasting value behind that the body can use to nourish itself. Anybody who tries to subsist on a diet of doughnuts is going to be sadly lacking in the sustenance needed to grow—at least to grow in the right way.

I'm afraid that this "doughnut principle" applies to churches that are more concerned with satisfying their members' spiritual "sweet tooth" than in providing nourishment for solid spiritual growth. Doughnut churches can be very popular, because what they offer tastes so good and there are a lot of people who are willing to sacrifice sustenance for succulence. But the church that wants to be authentic in its ministry must be bibliocentric, or Bible-centered, in its message. When the Word of God is not central to the church's proclamation, what you are left with is a spiritual doughnut shop.

WHAT WE NEED TO PROCLAIM

The Bible is amazingly clear and concise when it comes to the heart of the church's proclamation. Talking about God's Word in the context of the church's ministry takes us back to the Pastoral Epistles, the books of 1–2 Timothy and Titus that tell us how the church of God ought to function.

In this chapter I want us to consider several passages from 2 Timothy, particularly 2 Timothy 4:1–4, which addresses the church's proclamation. This is the Bible speaking of itself, for the apostle Paul instructed Timothy, the pastor at Ephesus, "I solemnly charge you in the presence of God and of Christ Jesus, who is to judge the living and the dead, and by His appearing and His kingdom: *preach the word*" (vv. 1–2a, italics added).

The Centrality of God's Word

I love the Bible's simplicity. When Paul told Timothy, and all the pastors and teachers who would follow him, to declare God's Word, it was like taking a Bible, putting it into his hand, and saying, "This is your message." I know that the whole Bible had not been revealed, written down, and conveniently bound together in one volume in Paul's day, but the message to the church is the same. Whatever else the church does, we need to proclaim the Word of God in its entirety.

In fact, we have no excuse whatsoever for failing to preach the Bible, because we *do* have the entire Word of God in our hands. Years before writing 2 Timothy, Paul had told the elders at Ephesus, "I did not shrink from declaring to you the whole purpose of God" (Acts 20:27). Any church that can say this is doing a lot of things right. The Word must be central.

That means a lot of other things must be peripheral. We are not told to preach our feelings, because feelings are notoriously unstable and offer no standard for truth. Neither are we told to preach human reasoning and intellect, which is flawed and limited and puffs people up with pride. The church isn't even called to preach good morals, in the sense of drawing up lists of dos and don'ts, because people have many different ideas of what's right and wrong, and what falls into the so-called gray area. What your momma told you may not be what my momma told me, in other words. So don't go around the church saying, "Well, my momma said."

The only issue that really matters is what God has said. His Word is the only standard and authority for the church. You may be saying, "Come on, Tony, that's obvious. Everybody knows the Bible is the church's standard."

No, not everybody does know that. And a lot of people who know it in their heads don't believe it in their hearts or practice it in their churches. It needs to be said again and again that the Bible is the church's only standard for the message we preach. Without it, the ballgame is over.

I say that because this subject reminds me of Bill Klem, the legendary baseball umpire of the early 1900s. Klem ran the game with an iron hand and wouldn't allow the rough characters of those days to intimidate him. One day a runner slid home on a close play with the game on the line.

Klem was on top of the play, but he didn't call it right away. The catcher and the runner both jumped up and started yelling, and both dugouts screamed at Klem to call the play their way. But Klem just studied the situation, until someone finally roared at him angrily, "Come on Klem! What is he, safe or out?"

Klem shot back, "He ain't nothin' till I say what he is!"

We live in a world where everybody wants to call the play their way. But the authoritative word has not been spoken until God has said it. And God has spoken in His Word. Our job is simply to deliver the message, the way a king's herald in medieval days would ride into a town, unroll the scroll of the king's message, and read it to the king's subjects, who were then obligated to obey. To preach is to declare what God has to say to His people, that they might understand the expectations and demands of the King.

The Power of Biblical Preaching

Biblical preaching confronts men and women with God through His Word, inspired and energized by the Holy Spirit, filtered through the personality of the pastor, so that the church will understand and respond to Him. Proclamation involves reading, explaining, and applying the Word.

Why does God want His church to preach the Word? Because we spend too much time listening to and studying the words of men, and too little time coming to grips with what God has said to us. You aren't going to find the world grappling with the Word, but there ought to be one place where you can go and get the real deal about what God thinks on the issues of life. That place is the church, the only entity on earth specifically charged with the responsibility of holding forth God's Word. The Bible is like a telescope. If you look through it, you can see the world far beyond. But if you just look at it, you don't see anything. The great danger is that the church will look at the Word and not through it.

So we need to make sure that the message we are delivering to the church is "Thus saith the Lord," not "Thus thinketh the pastor." I tell our people at church that if they want to know my personal opinions, call me at home, because in the pulpit my job is to deliver the King's message. I need to be evaluated as a pastor by how faithfully I preach the whole Word of God, not by whether I can move people to tears or shouts or impress them with my eloquence. The question is, Does what I say agree with what God says?

I want our church to be like the Bereans of Acts 17:11, whom Paul called "noble-minded" because "they received the word with great eagerness, examining the Scriptures daily to see whether these things were so." They didn't buy what Paul was preaching simply because he was an apostle. The Bereans' attitude was "Let's see if God really said what you just said that He said"—and Paul couldn't have been happier about the situation.

You have probably seen those metal stands at the airport that tell you whether a piece of luggage qualifies for carry-on. If you set your bag in the stand and it doesn't fit, you can't take it on the plane no matter what you may feel or think or what your momma told you. That metal rack is a fixed standard that doesn't budge, no matter how hard you try to stuff your oversized bag into its dimensions. You have to conform to the standard; it doesn't conform to you.

WHEN WE NEED TO PROCLAIM GOD'S WORD

Second Timothy 4:2 contains another needed word to the church concerning our biblical proclamation. Paul wrote, "Preach the word; be ready in season and out of season."

The Greek word *season* literally means "convenient." The answer to the "when" question concerning the church's proclamation of the Word is at any and every time, whether it's convenient or not.

Now that has a lot of applications. For a pastor it means to preach the Word no matter whether the congregation is saying amen or sitting and glaring. Preach the Word whether doing so reaps praise or anger. Preach the good parts that make everyone smile, but don't neglect the tough passages that have a hard message for God's people.

I remember hearing a story about George Beverly Shea, the long-time soloist with the Billy Graham organization. Shea was at a luncheon one day when the master of ceremonies spotted him and came over to invite him to sing. The man only had one request, that Shea not sing a gospel song since this was a secular gathering. Shea graciously declined, explaining that the only reason he had to sing was Jesus. Shea may not have sung that day, but he was ready to witness for Jesus even if the master of ceremonies thought it would be inconvenient.

If the devil can't silence the preaching of the Word through force, he'll try to silence it through intimidation. And, sad to say, it can happen in the church, because not every body of people that meets together under the banner of the church is really ready to hear and heed God's Word.

Why does God command His church to preach His Word all the time? Because there is no season and no time when God's people do not need to hear from Him. There is a reason that we don't go through the Bible once and then move on to something else. An old advertising slogan used to say, "You never outgrow your need for milk." I can't comment on the nutritional accuracy of that statement, but I can say with authority that we will never outgrow our need for God's Word. In fact, most of us need the inconvenient, "out of season" messages more than we might like to admit.

If you are looking for a church right now, or ever need to find one in the future, one good test by which to evaluate any church's ministry is the "seasons" test from 2 Timothy 4:2. That is, does the preacher handle the tough stuff from God's Word as well as the more easily accepted parts? Do any of his messages step on toes or make people uncomfortable?

I'm not talking about being disagreeable or hammering people with the Word. But the late preacher Vance Havner had it right when he said his job was "to comfort the afflicted and afflict the comfortable." If everything is "feel good" preaching, then you have a right to question whether the Bible is being preached in and out of season. Truth isn't always convenient.

With today's increased emphasis on "praise and worship" in the church, one of the things we have to be careful of is that the declaration of God's Word doesn't become devalued. With all the talented worship teams and catchy worship choruses the modern church has, it might be "convenient" for a pastor just to read a verse or two and offer a few thoughts at the end of the service and send the people home. But the church is not a performance center; it is a guardian of the truth.

Earlier in 2 Timothy, Paul wrote, "Retain the standard of sound words which you have heard from me. . . . Guard, through the Holy Spirit who dwells in us, the treasure which has been entrusted to you" (1:13–14), which is the Word of God. We have learned from 9/11 that we need to be on guard at all times, even when it's not convenient.

HOW WE NEED TO PROCLAIM GOD'S WORD

When the church is faithful to proclaim the Word of God, lives will be changed, because the Bible deals with the central issues of life through its principles and examples. We're not left in the dark as to how to preach the Word, thanks to our key verse in 2 Timothy 4:2 and another passage just above it in verse 16 of chapter 3.

There are a lot of important terms in these two texts that describe the effect the Word of God will have when it is applied to people's lives. Obviously, this doesn't have to be done exclusively by preaching, but the church's public proclamation of the Scriptures was Paul's concern in 2 Timothy 4, and that's our focus. In that context the apostle instructed Pastor Timothy, "Preach the word . . . reprove, rebuke, exhort, with great patience and instruction" (v. 2). Before we look at these terms, let's add 3:16: "All Scripture is inspired by God and profitable for teaching, for reproof, for correction, for training in righteousness."

There is some overlap in these two lists, but when we put them all together what emerges is an amazing picture of the power the Word has to shape and correct people's lives. The Word, and only the Word, has this power, because it is "inspired by God." From cover to cover the Bible is true or inerrant, which means without any error at all. Since the Author of Scripture is perfect, it is impossible for the product not to be perfect. The God of truth can only produce truth.

Proclaim the Word as Truth

So the fundamental answer to the question of how the Bible is to be preached and taught is that we are to present it as truth—absolute truth—without apologizing or stuttering. Remember that the church is "the pillar and support of the truth" (1 Timothy 3:15).

I was reminded of how little our culture cares for truth when I was contacted about being on the television program "Politically Incorrect," which has since been mercifully canceled. This was a panel discussion program with the goal of doing nothing but batting ideas around to see what everyone thought, and the more outrageous and twisted the opinions the better. Occasionally there were guests on the show who would try to defend some area of truth or decency, but they were usually ridiculed or shouted down. I turned down my invitation to appear, because the program wasn't interested in trying to get at the truth.

We know the Bible is true because this is the testimony God gives us concerning His Word. We need to keep coming back to Jesus' statement, "Your word is truth" (John 17:17). And because the Word is truth without any mixture of error, it can do what no other book can do. God's Word produces lasting results when it is faithfully and fully taught. Let's look at some of these results.

Preach the Word for Results

The apostle began with the word *reprove,* the same Greek word translated in a slightly different form in 2 Timothy 3:16 as "reproof." This means basically to tell someone what is wrong, not just to chastise but with a view to changing the wrong behavior. The Bible has an incredible ability to point up areas of sin and shortcoming in our lives. A preacher doesn't have to know what is happening with all the people in the congregation. All he has to do is preach the Word, and the Holy Spirit makes the application.

Timothy was also told to *rebuke* when necessary. This is a different word that means to bring a person under the conviction of guilt. See, a lot of folk know what's wrong in their lives. They just don't care that they're doing wrong and have never been brought under conviction to get it right. Jesus said that one of the Holy Spirit's jobs is to "convict" the world of sin and righteousness (see John 16:7–11). I don't have to try to work up people's emotions and play on their guilt to make them behave. The Word preached in the power of the Spirit is more than adequate to rebuke and convict.

Paul used a term in 2 Timothy 3:16 that is translated "correction," the only place this word occurs in the New Testament. It means to restore something to its original condition. The goal of the church's proclamation is to lead people into relationship and fellowship with God that restores man's original purpose and reverses sin's condemnation and corrupting influence in people's hearts.

The next word in the list of 2 Timothy 4:2 is *exhort.* Although reproof and rebuke are negative, this is the term for encouragement, the arm around the shoulder in support, urging the person along the right path. Biblical encouragement is more than just saying, "Hang in there" to someone. It has content because it is based in the Word. The best way I can encourage people as a pastor it to preach and teach God's Word faithfully and consistently.

The content of our rebuke, reproof, and encouragement is found in the words *instruction* (2 Timothy 4:2) and *teaching* (3:16). These are two forms of the same word, with the emphasis on what is taught and not so much on the method of teaching. We've already seen that the Scriptures themselves are the church's textbook for living.

Preach It with Authority

One other verse is important here because it provides a further clue as to how the church should proclaim the Word. Paul instructed Titus, his other pastoral representative, who was assigned to the island of Crete, "These things speak and exhort and reprove with all authority. Let no one disregard you" (Titus 2:15). The church's preaching must be done with authority because in the Bible we have the truth, the whole truth, and nothing but the truth.

We keep coming back to this issue of truth because it is rapidly becoming a lost concept in our world. And since 9/11 the intense focus on Islam and the Muslim world has given us a new truth challenge to contend with. This is the charge that we Christians are being arrogant and bigoted when we claim that the Bible is the only true Word of God. After all, the Muslims and other religious people have their own "holy books" too.

We could talk about all the evidence that supports the Bible's truth claims, but we'll save that for a study of the Bible itself. The point here is that what the Bible calls authoritative preaching of the Word is now considered by the world at large to be biased and even hate-filled preaching.

Actually, this problem isn't all that new, because Paul and Timothy also lived in a world that was hostile to absolute truth. First-century Ephesus was a culture of relativism, but Paul's instruction to the church there was to preach the Word when people liked it and when they didn't, when they wanted to hear the truth and when they didn't.

No pastor who is preaching the Word needs to apologize for the message. People need an absolute and absolutely reliable standard by which to measure their lives. I illustrated this at church one Sunday morning by reading the time on my watch and then asking several people in the congregation what time they had. One person's watch agreed with mine, but others were several minutes different. One guy's watch wasn't even close to the time, making me wonder where he had been.

But the point I made was that it didn't really matter whether we all agreed among ourselves, because none of us on our own had the exact time. That is kept by the government's atomic clock in Colorado, which sets the official time for the nation. Without that we could argue all day about the right time. But once the standard is set, we have to adjust to it. The church must proclaim God's Word with authority so everyone is on the same page when it comes to God's standard.

WHY WE NEED TO PROCLAIM IT

Having seen what, when, and how the church is to carry out its ministry of proclamation, we're ready to answer the why of the matter.

Why must we preach the Word in all of its convicting and teaching power? Because people need to hear the truth and feed on healthy spiritual doctrine, and because they aren't likely to get this if left on their own.

This is the positive side of Paul's admonition concerning the necessity of preaching the Word: "For the time will come when they will not endure sound doctrine; but wanting to have their ears tickled, they will accumulate for themselves teachers in accordance to their own desires, and will turn away their ears from the truth and will turn aside to myths" (2 Timothy 4:3–4).

People Need to Hear the Truth

Human nature is such that people will get itchy ears and begin to gravitate toward teachers who will only say what they want to hear. If all you care about is attracting a crowd, start a "doughnut" church whose primary goal is to make people feel good and be happy about themselves. In a church like this people can get any kind of doughnut they want, with as much glaze over the truth as they want, and it will all taste sweet. But the result will be a group of people on a temporary "sugar high" who will stumble and falter someday for lack of solid spiritual nourishment.

Now I'm not saying it will always be easy to preach the truth, or to hear and obey it. When my granddaughter and I make our morning run to the doughnut shop, there is usually a line of people ahead us crowding in to get their sugar fix. But did you ever notice that you don't see long lines at the health food stores?

There is a message here for the church, because the Greek word for *sound* in verse 3 means "healthy." By and large, people won't gravitate toward either healthy food or healthy doctrine if left on their own. That's why the church has to make sure that there is one place where people are being fed a healthy, balanced diet of the truth as it is found in God's Word.

People Need Healthy Spiritual Food

Whenever I teach this passage I think of our trips home to my parents' house in Baltimore. My momma is still determined to make sure that I eat right, and she doesn't care one bit that I am a grown man and grandfather who is capable of making his own choices. When we sit down to eat, she'll put a bowl of squash or some other nasty stuff I don't like on the table, and may the Lord have mercy if I try to pass it along without taking some.

The fried chicken will come by, and you can be sure I get my thighs. The potato salad, green beans, and hot bread come around, and I'm in business. Then the squash comes and I try to pass it on. But if momma sees me, she says, "Boy, what do you think you're doing?"

I try to protest. "Momma, I'm a grown man and I don't want any squash. I know what I like and what I don't like, and I don't like squash."

To which my mother will say, "You know what, you are in my house now." She will then take the bowl and start spooning this stuff onto my plate. And she always puts more on my plate than I would have if I had just gone ahead and done it myself. Then she hits me with the clinching line, "And you'd better eat it all, too, because it's good for you." I know that, but if it were up to me my meal would be fried chicken and the other stuff without worrying about what's good for me.

When you come to church there is nothing wrong with getting some chicken and mashed potatoes, but you need some squash too because it's good for you. We need to hear the parts of the Word that we may not prefer because the Holy Spirit uses them to "meddle" in our lives. But if we don't get the truth in church, God help us, because we aren't going to get it in the world. The world can't digest healthy doctrine, and there are plenty of teachers out there ready to sugarcoat the truth, even in the name of God.

There will always be things in the Word of God that go against what we would like to believe, or what we have been taught. There may be something we want to do, and would do too, if it weren't for the Word standing there saying, "Thou shalt not." People with ears itching for what they want to hear and what agrees with their prejudices can always find a teacher willing to scratch the itch, to make the Word fit conveniently into their plans and their ideas.

But the nature of truth is that it doesn't matter whether you agree or what you think. Truth doesn't change, so the church's job is to help people keep their ears turned toward the truth—which, by the way, will not only scratch the *real* itch inside but satisfy with solid spiritual nourishment.

Changing the analogy, the church's proclamation should hold up the mirror of God's Word to our faces so we can see what we really look like and make any adjustments necessary (see James 1:23–25). Let's make sure that we are holding up the Word of truth for all to see. "Preach the word" is God's charge to the church.

9

THE WITNESS OF THE CHURCH

I was in New York City in the summer of 2002 when a special ceremony was held to honor the firefighters and other rescuers who had put their lives on the line during the terrorist attacks of 9/11. It was a very serious and somber ceremony as the city remembered all those who lost their lives seeking to rescue others on that terrible day because they were in a life-and-death situation.

We have all heard the stories of people who laid aside their own comfort and safety and took great risks to save lives, because a lot of people were facing certain doom and the rescuers knew they could not simply stand by and watch people perish. There was too much at stake to be casual about the situation. The 9/11 rescuers mobilized themselves because they knew that many people would either live or die based on their efforts.

People who are facing certain disaster need a rescuer to lead them out of harm's way, no matter what the cost or inconvenience to the rescuer. And people who are facing certain spiritual disaster without Jesus Christ also need someone to lead them to safety, which is to the cross of Jesus Christ where sin is paid for and forgiven. This is why God has called and mobilized the church as a "rescue unit"— to go out into the world and be His witnesses, to turn people on their way to hell toward heaven. "You shall be My witnesses," Jesus said (Acts 1:8).

It is the local church's job to equip its members to go out among the dying and bring them a message of life. It is our calling as followers of Jesus Christ to lead lost people through the fire and smoke to the safety of the cross. You are never further from the heart of God than you are when you are silent to your unsaved friends and loved ones about the gospel and the eternal life that Jesus gives. And you are never closer to the heart of God than when you are telling others how they can be saved and bringing them to the Savior. Just as people are trained in CPR so they can rescue people who are in crisis, so the church is God's primary training ground to equip His people in the art of spiritual CPR.

We are going to see that evangelism is a priority with God. But the problem is that evangelism is often not a priority with God's people. One reason is that being a witness is not about you and me and what we want God to do for us. It's not about our job, our finances, our children, and so on. In other words, evangelism runs counter to our natural tendency to see to our needs first. There is certainly a place for all of the things I mentioned, but being a witness is about that lost neighbor and unsaved co-worker who are in a burning building, so to speak, and will never make it out alive unless someone helps them.

PRAYING FOR LOST PEOPLE

Having just read that people are lost and on their way to hell unless we reach them, and that God wants us to be His witnesses, you might expect me to say, "So let's get out there in the unsaved world and start witnessing."

Well, we need to do that, to be sure. But God has an order within His priority of evangelism. The heading of this section tells you where we're going first, so let's look at what Paul wrote to Timothy, his spiritual son and pastoral representative in Ephesus. In 1 Timothy 2 the apostle laid down key principles for the church that wants to reach its world for Jesus Christ. Notice Paul's emphasis in the opening verses:

> First of all, then, I urge that entreaties and prayers, petitions and thanksgivings, be made on behalf of all men, for kings and all who are in authority, so that we may lead a tranquil and quiet life in all godliness and dignity. This is good and acceptable in the sight of God our Savior, who desires all men to be saved and to come to the knowledge of the truth. (vv. 1–4)

Before we get into the specifics of these and the following verses, please note God's desire that all people come to the knowledge of Christ. Peter said of God's desire, "The Lord is not slow about His promise, as some count slowness, but is patient toward you, not wishing for any to perish but for all to come to repentance" (2 Peter 3:9).

There are biblical and theological reasons why everyone is not saved, because God in His grace has called His elect to Himself. But He never told us to try to figure out who the elect are. Our job is to present the gospel freely to all, because God's heart is for all the lost.

I'm pointing this out because some Christians give the impression that once they got saved, God went out of the salvation business. I don't know anyone who would actually say that, but Christians who cannot find the time or the concern to share the gospel with anyone else are saying to unsaved people by their actions, "I got my salvation, hope you get yours."

Praying with the Right Passion

So what does the God who wants all people to be saved want His people to do about it? He wants us to pray for a lost world "first of all." These are priority words. That's why I want to begin by considering the church's prayer ministry in relation to evangelism. We have already talked about the Great Commission and the importance of going into all the world as part of our disciple-making ministry. I don't really believe I need to take a lot of time trying to convince you that the church is supposed to go.

But I do believe that our biblical calling to *pray* before we go and as we go is sadly lacking in emphasis in the church at large. We'll talk about going later, but what is needed in the church today is a renewed understanding that God wants prayer to be at the center of the church's life and evangelistic efforts. In fact, the priority of prayer is such that it comes before a lot of other programs and projects the church gets caught up in that, when all is said and done, have an inward, "us"-centered focus.

The four words Paul used in 1 Timothy 2:1 to describe prayer are instructive in helping us understand how God wants us to pray evangelistically. The word *entreaties* is related to a word that means "to need" or "to lack," so entreaties are prayers that address a need. What greater need can unsaved people have than their need for Christ? Anything else the church can do for the lost will only last for this life. But if these people die without Christ, they are lost for eternity.

Next, the word *prayers* is the general word for the act of prayer, and it refers to our worship before God. In fact, this word always points to God when it is used in Scripture. Praying for the lost is an act of worship before God, which puts it on a higher level. When the church prays evangelistically, we are bringing people before the throne of God, asking Him to open their hearts.

The third word of 1 Timothy 2:1 is *petitions*. These are requests that we make on behalf of others, which require that we get close enough to people to know what their needs are and feel their pain. And *thanksgivings* simply means to be grateful, which certainly involves thanking God for His saving grace in Christ and for what He is going to do in response to the prayers of His people.

When we put it all together, what God wants from our prayers for evangelism is that we pray for all people, but not just in some general sense of "Lord, I want to pray for the world." Our prayers should reflect our deep concern for the lost as real people and the priority that we have given to their need of Christ. A "Lord, help the lost" kind of prayer is not going to move the heart of God.

Since God's priority in prayer is evangelism instead of us and our concerns, we may have an answer as to why more of God's people are not seeing more of their prayers answered. It's because they have their priorities out of order. People who are facing a life-or-death situation need a rescuer, and you can only become a rescuer when you put aside your agenda.

Praying for the Right People

The Bible makes us understand that no one is left out when the church goes to prayer for the lost. This is obvious from the "all men" at the end of 1 Timothy 2:1. When we pray evangelistically for unsaved people, we are saying it's not enough that we are saved. We want to help more dying people get into the lifeboat and be saved.

This reminds me of the terrible *Titanic* disaster in which fifteen hundred people drowned in the cold waters of the Atlantic Ocean after the great ship went down in April 1912. Among the many tragic things that happened on that famous night, one was that many of the lifeboats rowing away from the *Titanic* had room for more people. But those who were safe in the boats didn't want to turn around and go back to save more victims because they were afraid too many people might try to get in and capsize the boats. According to the story, only one lifeboat turned around and picked up six people, when there was room in the boats for many more.

It's one thing to try to rescue people who know they are dying. The *Titanic* victims in the water were screaming for help because they knew their lives were ebbing away. But it's just as critical to rescue people who don't realize their danger and aren't even crying out for help. Most lost people in our world are not screaming out for rescue, but they are drowning as surely as those people treading water near the *Titanic* were drowning.

Of course, the issue in evangelism isn't whether those who are drowning know they are in trouble and are crying out for help. The issue is that they are lost and facing eternity in hell without Christ, and the church has the responsibility to reach them with the gospel. So the important thing is not so much what is happening in the ocean, but what's happening in the lifeboats that are on the ocean.

Too many of us are too comfortable in our "Jesus lifeboat." Instead of the church preparing its members to reach out to other people who are still in the water and pulling them into the boat, we have settled in for the ride to heaven and are busy coming up with ways to make the trip more comfortable. We go to church each week and worship God because we are saved and safe, forgetting that the lifeboat is not yet full.

The church needs to be stirred up in the area of evangelism, and the thing that will stir God's people more than any evangelistic "pep talks" or guilt trips or programs is prayer. If you ask me, "How can I get a burden for lost people and overcome my fear of witnessing?" my answer would be to start praying. Pray for unsaved family members, friends, and co-workers by name. Ask God to break your heart over their condition and give you "divine appointments" to share Christ with them and the boldness to speak for Him.

And, by the way, if you feel fearful at times you are not alone. Even Paul, the great evangelist, asked the Ephesians to pray that he would have the boldness necessary to proclaim the gospel. Paul's prayer request is worth quoting here because it would make a great prayer for you to pray: "Pray . . . that utterance may be given to me in the opening of my mouth, to make known with boldness the mystery of the gospel . . . that in proclaiming it I may speak boldly, as I ought to speak" (Ephesians 6:19–20).

I'm convinced that churches have to do a much more deliberate and thorough job of teaching their members how to pray for lost people, and then set the example by making evangelistic prayer a part of the church's regular ministry. One way you can begin to pray for lost people is to ask them if they have needs or concerns you can pray for. It's pretty hard to turn down a caring friend who wants to pray for you.

You see, our unsaved friends and family members may not know that they are lost and on their way to a Christless eternity. But they do know that they have family and financial hassles to deal with. They know they are lonely or frustrated or they need help with their kids. In other words, people have felt needs that we can pray about and help them with. And God can use your intervention to reverse a situation that seems hopeless, just as a football coach in the pros can appeal a close call that goes against his team.

Perhaps you have seen how the referee goes over to a special television monitor, puts on a set of earphones, and watches an instant replay of the call. He is then free to reverse a call by any of the officials if that is warranted, which means that the play isn't really over until the judge has made his ruling. Don't ever give up praying for people, because God can overrule any human power or situation to soften people's hearts toward the gospel.

The Bible says that Christians are no longer to live for themselves (see 2 Corinthians 5:15). Many of us are not seeing the power of God at work because we're living for ourselves when God wants us to have a heart for others that's as big as the needy world we live in. When we start praying for people, we won't have a hard time reaching out to the spiritually dying and making room for them in the lifeboat, because we will realize that the church's witness is a life-and-death issue.

Praying for the Right Conditions

At first glance, Paul's request in 1 Timothy 2:2 may not seem to fit with the theme of praying for the lost. The apostle urged the church to pray in particular "for kings and all who are in authority, so that we may lead a tranquil and quiet life in all godliness and dignity."

But it makes perfect sense in the context because it's clear that the main reason Paul wanted us to pray for a peaceful environment is to enhance the spread of the gospel. Over the past ten years we have witnessed enough riots and rebel attacks and dislocations of entire populations to know that as a rule, social and political upheaval do not make a conducive environment in which to share the gospel. In fact, in many of the world's troubled countries the most endangered people during a riot or attack, and among the first to be evacuated, are the missionaries in that area.

So a priority reason that we are to pray for "domestic tranquility," as the preamble to the U.S. Constitution puts it, is to enhance the spread of the gospel. The blessing of being in America is that we can talk about God freely. Now don't misunderstand. Domestic peace is not absolutely necessary to the spread of the gospel, as we have witnessed in countries where the church is growing despite oppression and persecution. But I don't know anyone who wishes or prays for turmoil and persecution so the gospel can grow. Paul certainly didn't. The hostile environment in which Paul ministered added pain and burden to his work, and he had no problem telling the church to pray for quiet and tranquil lives.

Another benefit of praying for peace in the context of evangelism is that it helps you to see your life and the world from God's perspective—a perspective that we don't come by naturally. If you ever used those old 3-D glasses they used to give out at special movies, you know that the audience needed them to see what was happening on the screen. God wants His church to see the world through His "glasses," because without them we can get things out of focus and begin to think that He is blessing us with peace for our enjoyment alone.

This prayer for tranquility also applies to other spheres of authority. Pray for peace at work and favor with your employer so that you will have opportunity to share Christ without people getting upset. Pray for an environment at home, in your extended family, and in your neighborhood that is conducive to spreading the gospel.

Let me make an important distinction between this kind of tranquility and the false peace that surrounds many unbelievers. We said earlier that few non-Christians in our culture realize they are lost and heading toward hell. This is because Satan has constructed an amusement park of worldly distractions to keep them from focusing and realizing that they are drowning souls. If there are enough television programs, films, sports, and parties to keep people amused, they may never wake up to the fact that they are lost.

Many unbelievers are like a child at an amusement park who is having so much fun that he doesn't realize he has been separated from his parents and is lost. A child in this condition needs to stop, wake up, and look around to see that he is totally alone. Then he is ready for help. So there's nothing wrong with praying that God will "trouble the waters" for unbelievers to bring them to themselves and to Christ.

Praying for souls is like holding a magnifying glass over a piece of paper on a sunny day. The glass concentrates the sun's rays on the paper and sets the paper on fire. The glass doesn't increase the sun's power, but focuses it on a particular location. That's what corporate prayer does, which is why prayer is a priority in evangelism.

GOING TO REACH LOST PEOPLE

Whenever the Bible addresses any subject, it does so with perfect balance. We can see that in 1 Timothy 2. Paul said to begin with prayer for the lost, but he didn't say that this is all the church has to do. In verses 5–7 he drew on his personal example to show that praying for the lost must be accompanied by going to the lost with the good news of salvation. This is what I call pray-ers—that is, people who pray—becoming proclaimers.

A Great Savior to Proclaim

We have the essence of the gospel in verse 5, where Paul wrote, "For there is one God, and one mediator also between God and men, the man Christ Jesus." The Word of God tells us that there is only one way to reach God, and that is through Jesus Christ. This basic truth has become a flash point of controversy because since 9/11, everyone is bending over backward to show that we're all just one big family and that Christians and Muslims in particular worship the same God.

No way. It doesn't matter if the world thinks the gospel is narrow or intolerant. But neither Buddha, Mohammed, nor any other religious figure can bridge the gap between sinful people and a holy God. That chasm from hell to heaven was bridged by Jesus, and only by Jesus, on the cross.

I like the way Job put it in reference to the gulf between him as a human being and God: "There is no umpire between us, who may lay his hand upon us both" (Job 9:33). Job was painfully aware of his inability to stand before a holy God, and lamented the lack of an "umpire," or mediator, who was qualified to step in.

But now that need has been met in Jesus Christ. He fits the criteria perfectly because He is both holy God and a sinless man. Paul continued in 1 Timothy to describe this uniquely qualified mediator: "[Jesus] gave Himself as a ransom for all, the testimony given at the proper time" (2:6). To ransom people means to pay the price to set them free, to rescue them from their predicament. He came to rescue people, and if you and I aren't in the rescuing business, we aren't in Jesus' business. He said, "As the Father has sent Me, I also send you" (John 20:21). Where did the Father send the Son? He sent Him into the world to hang out with sinners and bring them to Himself.

The sinking of the *Titanic* was a tragedy on more than one count. Not only did people die unnecessarily in the water after the ship went down, but you may know that the accident didn't have to happen in the first place. The *Titanic's* radio operator received a number of messages from other vessels, warning of the danger of icebergs. But none of the messages except the last one was delivered because the radio operator didn't think they were serious enough to be relayed to the captain. So the *Titanic's* crew didn't know that a life-and-death situation lay ahead of them—and because the message wasn't delivered in time, the ship and those fifteen hundred lives were lost.

I need to ask you some hard questions. Do you have relatives, friends, neighbors, or co-workers on their way to hell today who could legitimately say someday that you never told them about Jesus and how they could be saved? How many people could say to you at the judgment, "I worked next to you for twenty years, and you never told me about Jesus"? Or "I was family, and yet you never opened your mouth to tell me that I was lost!" It's also important to ask if your church is equipping you to be a spiritual rescuer. If not, something is amiss.

If we really believe Acts 4:12, then there is no excuse for not telling others about Jesus. Speaking of Jesus Christ (see v. 10), Peter said, "There is salvation in no one else; for there is no other name under heaven that has been given among men by which we must be saved."

A Great Message to Deliver

Paul believed that message and was glad to say that he was "a preacher and an apostle" (1 Timothy 2:7). A preacher has a message to proclaim, and the word *apostle* itself means a "sent one," so Paul's very "job title" showed that he was to go out with the gospel. We are not apostles, but we *are* "sent ones" because our Savior has commissioned us and sent us into the world with the word of eternal life.

If you are a saved person and thus a part of the church of Jesus Christ, then it doesn't matter what your job description is or the title on your business card. Your true assignment is to be a witness for Jesus Christ cleverly disguised as a salesperson, teacher, physician, college student, homemaker, or whatever you do. Why? Because God says helping others to know Him is a "first of all" priority for the church.

But if evangelism is far down on your church's priority list, then you shouldn't be surprised if you don't see God showing up in power in your midst. We can't turn God's agenda upside down and expect Him to move among us. If you have been rescued and brought into the lifeboat, reach out and pull someone else in.

Many years ago and many pounds ago, I used to be a water safety instructor, the person who trains lifeguards. I became a lifeguard first and then moved on to the instructor position.

Let me tell you why I decided to become a water safety instructor. When I was little, I almost drowned. The incident is as real to me today as it was the day it happened, and I can still see it clearly. I was in water over my head and my toes were not touching. I tried to push myself up so I could yell for help, but I was choking on water and couldn't get the word "Help!" out.

The other people in the water might have thought I was playing around, but one person took me seriously and reached into the water to pull me out of what had become a life-and-death situation. After knowing what it felt like to be drowning and have someone deliver me, I wanted to be a deliverer of others so that if they began to drown someone would be there for them just as someone was there for me.

If God has reached down and pulled you out of the miry clay of sin, then you have the responsibility to be a deliverer for somebody else. All of us have the time. It takes three hours to watch that football game, but only a few minutes to pray for lost souls. We will go to great lengths of inconvenience and expense for an evening of entertainment, but going to a friend's house with the gospel is free. The issue is never our busyness, but what is "first of all" in our hearts.

A Game to Enter

Jesus is not looking for spectators, but folk who are "players." These are the ones who are in the game, praying for the unsaved and willing to go out into the world to reach them. It's easy to have our priorities straight on Sunday morning when we are together in God's house praising Him. But we need to take our prayers and our actions outside the doors, getting on our knees before God on behalf of unsaved people and then moving our feet to go to them with the gospel.

You may say, "But I'm not a preacher. I haven't been to seminary." That's fine, because you don't have to be a professional theologian to tell someone about Christ. If you can share your testimony and open your Bible to share the gospel, you can help bring a lost person to new birth in Christ.

Peter and John told those who tried to silence them, "We cannot stop speaking about what we have seen and heard" (Acts 4:20). Have you seen God do anything in your life worth talking about? Heard any good news lately that you think someone else needs to hear? Then you are qualified to be a witness for Jesus Christ. He said, "The harvest is plentiful, but the workers are few" (Matthew 9:37). There are plenty of sinners, but God says He has a hard time finding enough saints who are willing to get serious about His harvest.

Paul came back to the priority of prayer in 1 Timothy 2:8, where he instructed: "Therefore I want the men in every place to pray, lifting up holy hands, without wrath and dissension." The emphasis here is on those who are leading public prayer in the church assembly. This is a picture of the church at prayer, which Paul said needs to be done with the right attitude because this is not about our private disputes or gripes. This verse and verse 1 are like bookends that hold this great section of Scripture together. The church is to pray for all people, because God's desire is that all people come to the knowledge of the truth.

According to Jesus, "There will be more joy in heaven over one sinner who repents than over ninety-nine righteous persons who need no repentance" (Luke 15:7). If heaven throws a celebration each time a sinner comes to Christ, make sure that you are getting in on the rejoicing by taking someone to heaven with you.

I remember seeing an old World War II–type movie in which a bunch of soldiers' wives had gathered to greet a planeload of troops coming home from the war. As each soldier stepped off the plane and his wife spotted him, there were hugs and kisses and tears of joy. But some women waited and waited, and when the plane was empty they were still looking for their beloved husbands, who weren't there because they had not survived the war. One woman ran to the plane and asked the crew, "Is there anybody else on the plane?"

"No, there's nobody else."

The woman put her face in her hands and began to sob.

Don't let it be that people you want to see in heaven fail to make it because you never got around to praying for them and telling them about Christ. We are not responsible to save people. Only Christ can save. But we can and must be His witnesses. We can pray and go in the confidence that we are putting first things first as God would have us do. And when we act on God's priorities, we can expect His help, power, and blessing.

THE
IMPACT
OF THE
CHURCH

The AIDS virus has become a scourge that threatens to wipe out an entire generation in parts of the world. AIDS is fundamentally a breakdown in the body's immune system. As the HIV virus attacks and incapacitates the immune system, the body becomes vulnerable to a number of other diseases. A cold can become pneumonia, and an otherwise minor infection can become life-threatening. Many AIDS sufferers do not die of the disease itself, but of AIDS-related complications.

What is true of the AIDS virus is true on every level of our society. Our spiritual immune system has been badly damaged, with the result that cultural colds have become societal pneumonia, and minor cultural infections have now become life-threatening. And none of the political and societal medications being applied to the problem is working.

But there is hope, because God has established an immune

system for the culture called the church. The disease of spiritual AIDS, or sin, threatens to debilitate society, but the church and only the church can counteract the destructive effects of this terrible virus. In relation to the culture, the church's job is to repel the viruses of sin that damage a civilization. But if the immune system is weak, then we ought not to be surprised that colds and sniffles in the culture wind up becoming cultural pneumonia.

You see, as goes the church so goes the society. If we want strong communities, then there must be strong churches at the heart of those communities. A healthy community needs an intact immune system standing against the evil that would debilitate and destroy society. But the church's calling to impact the world has become a lot more challenging today. One reason is that the world's attitude toward the church has taken a drastically negative turn since the simpler times of the 1940s and '50s, when churches were generally considered to be pillars in the community.

I have a friend whose father was a pastor in a classic "Norman Rockwell" kind of Midwestern town in the 1950s. When the church built a new building, a neighbor came over with his hammer to help out because, as he told the pastor, "I wouldn't live in a community without a church." And he worked side-by-side with the church's men to put up the building. The interesting thing is that this man was a hardened unbeliever who refused to attend the church, but he realized that having a church in the community was a positive thing.

Things have changed today! Now we read about cities and towns all over the country refusing to allow churches to build or add on to their present buildings. As I write this, there is a major legal battle being waged at the national level to try to recapture some very basic civil and legal rights for churches. Churches that used to be looked on as an asset to their communities are now considered a tax, noise, and traffic liability—and people are saying, "Not in my backyard."

It's no wonder the church is often confused about its role. Back in the 1920s, after the fundamentalists lost the battle for the mainline denominations and their schools, which went liberal almost without exception, the fundamentalists retreated from the world and established their own denominations, schools, parachurch agencies, and mission boards. Many of us as Bible-believing Christians today are the product and the beneficiaries of this movement, but the great challenge ever since is how the church is supposed to relate to the broader society.

UNIQUE PEOPLE
WITH A UNIQUE PURPOSE

The Bible teaches that the people of God are unique. Peter called us "a spiritual house for a holy priesthood" and "a chosen race, a royal priesthood, a holy nation, a people for God's own possession" (1 Peter 2:5, 9). That makes us different and set apart, yet we are also created for "good works" (Ephesians 2:10) that impact the world around us.

Two Harmful Extremes

There is a lot of confusion here. Some churches are so heavenly minded they are of no earthly good. They sing, shout, and pray while the community outside continues to spiral downward into social and moral decay. People in churches like this love God, but they don't take that love outside the church's walls to the neighborhood. They're basically hiding from the world and its ugliness. There doesn't appear to be any relationship between this heavenly gathering and the hellish environment outside its walls. Churches like this are looking toward eternity, but are of little benefit in history.

The other extreme is what has happened to so many churches since the 1920s battles. That is, they have become so earthly minded that they are no heavenly good. In other words, they've become secularized, surrendering the truth of the gospel and the demands of the life hereafter for the here-and-now. Churches like this have turned the house of God into a political forum rather than a place where people learn the divine viewpoint. Heaven can't use these churches because they are not heavenly in their thinking.

Both of these extremes are wrong. The church is made up of people who are called to live out heaven's values in the midst of a very unheavenly world. We receive instructions from above, with our feet firmly planted here below. We are to think heavenly, and let it show in our earthly walk. We are looking for the return of Jesus, but we have a lot to do while we're waiting for Him to come.

Doing Jesus' Business

Jesus Himself expressed the biblical viewpoint for the church in His parable of the man who went away on a long journey and left his estate with his servants to manage. In Luke's version of the parable the owner of the estate told his servants, "Do business with this until I come back" (19:13).

Here is the balance the church needs to strike. The man's servants knew he was coming back, so they had to live in light of that certainty. But, at the same time, they were left with his resources and his charge, "Do business with this." The answer was not to sit down and do nothing until the master returned or to get all wrapped up in the business of life and forget that he was coming back.

Later in 1 Peter 2, the apostle struck this balance with a marvelous description of how the church should impact the world while staying true to Christ: "I urge you as aliens and strangers to abstain from fleshly lusts which wage war against the soul. Keep your behavior excellent among the Gentiles, so that in the thing in which they slander you as evildoers, they may *because of your good deeds, as they observe them,* glorify God in the day of visitation" (vv. 11–12, italics added).

Notice the heavenly part of this exhortation. We are "aliens" down here. This world is only a seventy- or eighty-year pit stop on the way home. A former inmate was once asked how he survived in prison. "Oh, that's easy. All the other guys on my cellblock made themselves at home. They put up pictures and decorated their cells. But I wasn't planning on staying there, so I never made myself at home."

We aren't home either, so while we're passing through this world we are called to be holy, or set apart, in body and spirit. And yet, our lives are to be so influential that non-Christians can't help but glorify God for what they see in us.

The measure of any church is twofold: how we grow our members internally and the difference we make in the society externally. It's one thing to feel good when we leave the Lord's house on Sunday. But it's another thing to live from Monday to Saturday in such a way that we influence the community where the Lord's house is located.

THE SALT OF THE EARTH

Now we're ready to answer the important question of how the church's influence in society is intended to function. One of the most concise yet comprehensive statements on this subject is from the lips of Jesus in Matthew 5:13–16. In the Sermon on the Mount, the Lord used two key metaphors to communicate the impact He wants us (the church) to make for Him. The first one is salt.

Salt's Preserving Influence

You could probably recite the first half of verse 13 from memory. Jesus told us, "You are the salt of the earth." (The second half of the verse adds a needed word about the importance of retaining our influence, which we'll deal with in a moment.)

By declaring His people the salt of the earth, Jesus was making a clear statement about the decaying condition of this world and the role of Christians in delaying the decay. Of course, salt has been used as a preservative for thousands of years. Rubbing it into a piece of meat helps to preserve the meat from decay, because salt is an antibacterial agent.

Roman soldiers in biblical days were also said to receive their pay in salt. The value of salt in a world with no refrigeration was pretty obvious. Salt's value became part of the language, which we can see today in the word *salary*. Check the dictionary and you'll see that *salary* is a derivative of the word *salt*. You're familiar with the expression that so-and-so is not worth his salt. A person who didn't do his job right didn't receive his full allocation of salt.

Jesus put His church on earth to act as a preserving influence on a rotting world, to slow down the decay of sin. If Jesus had nothing on earth for His people to do, He would have taken us out of here the moment we trusted Him as Savior. Evil ought to slow down and take notice when it gets in the vicinity of the church, because we are being salt.

But, as someone has pointed out, salt can't do its job when it is sitting in the shaker. The church gathered in the house of God is salt in the shaker. When the doors open and we go out into the world, that's when the shaker should get turned up to spread the salt where it is needed. It's easy to be salt in the shaker, because we're all together and doing the same thing. But the decay is out there in the streets, and that's where we need to infiltrate the evil and spread the preserving salt of God's kingdom and His righteousness.

If our neighborhoods are going to be better, and if our families are going to be stronger, then the salt must be at work. I'm not talking about theoretical stuff. Every time God uses His people to bring a sinner to Christ, set a young person on the right course, rebuild a disintegrating family, or take a public stand for righteousness on an important issue, the salt is doing its job. Every local church needs to ask itself whether its community is better, stronger, and spiritually healthier because that church is located there.

When Salt Becomes Tasteless

Jesus finished His illustration on salt by saying, "But if the salt has become tasteless, how can it be made salty again? It is no longer good for anything, except to be thrown out and trampled under foot by men" (Matthew 5:13b). In the culture of Jesus' day when salt was so crucial in preserving food, there was nothing worse than salt that had lost its usefulness.

A lot of people wonder about this statement because sodium

chloride is a stable compound that cannot lose its saltiness or taste. What Jesus is referring to here is the fact that a lot of the salt in biblical days was distilled from marshes and other places where it was mixed with all manner of impurities. When the salt was used up, the impurities would remain and render the mixture useless. There was nothing to do but toss it out on the ground.

Tasteless salt was also "trampled under foot" because in biblical days people mixed gypsum with water to make a paste for patching holes in their roofs. The paste was solidified with salt, which was then good for nothing else because it was mixed with gypsum, which is bitter. The bitterness of the gypsum canceled out the saltiness of the salt.

This salt was trampled underfoot because in Jesus' days the homes in Israel had flat roofs that were the center of a lot of activity. People could fight from the rooftops, and they were the scene of many social occasions such as wedding receptions. Israelis used their roofs the way we use a veranda or porch.

All of that walking on the roofs would create holes, because the roofs were usually just earth. The gypsum and salt mixture was used to patch the holes, so the salt would literally be trampled underfoot by people. This is a graphic picture of God's people becoming so diluted by the world that we lose our impact and the world walks right over us without feeling any effect.

And, by the way, the church doesn't have to fall into gross sin to lose its distinctive impact. When the church becomes so aligned with the Republicans or the Democrats that you can't tell the difference between the church and the party, the church compromises its impact and the world either disregards us or takes us for granted. To be sure, the church needs to have a voice in the public square. But we cannot allow God's kingdom agenda to be subjugated to social or political agendas. If we lose our saltiness, the culture is left without a righteous, preserving influence.

The Bible provides us with a powerful example of what righteous people can do to preserve and impact a society and, at the same time, a tragic example of what happens when those people fail to be salt. Both sides of the coin are crucial, because after saying His people are the salt of the earth, Jesus added, "But if the salt has become tasteless, how can it be made salty again? It is no longer good for anything, except to be thrown out and trampled under foot by men" (Matthew 5:13b).

The example is found in Genesis 18:16–19:38, the story of Abraham's negotiations with the Lord over the wicked cities of Sodom and Gomorrah and their destruction. These cities were located in the vicinity of the Dead Sea, which is so full of salt that nothing can live in it. I've been to the Dead Sea and have seen cakes of salts floating on top of the water. Some people even think the ruins of Sodom may be buried under the Dead Sea, which is interesting given the connection between salt and the story of Sodom.

Genesis 18 begins with a visit that God and two angels made in human form to Abraham as he sat by his tent. As the three got ready to leave, they looked toward Sodom because the plan was to destroy it (see vv. 16–21). The very fact that God revealed His intention to Abraham ahead of time and allowed Abraham to intervene on behalf of Sodom shows how the righteous can exert an influence on society. And yet, Lot's failure to exert any discernible righteous influence on Sodom shows what happens when a believer's salt becomes tasteless.

I'll summarize the story from here because it's the bottom line I want us to see. Abraham entered into intense negotiations with God to spare the city, in part because Abe's nephew Lot and his family were living in Sodom. You'll recall that God finally agreed to spare Sodom if just ten righteous people could be found in this city that some experts say could have had as many as 500,000 people.

With the negotiations over, the two angels who had come to Abraham went on to Sodom, and Genesis 19 details the sad attempt to rescue Lot and his family. This attempt ended with Lot's sons-in-law laughing at his warning of judgment, Lot's wife looking back and turning into a pillar of salt because her heart was still in Sodom, and Lot's two daughters entering into incest with him and producing two nations of people who became Israel's bitter enemies.

Now the question is, Why were Sodom and Gomorrah destroyed? Most people would say because of the homosexuality and all the perversion that went with it. Well, that's only half of the answer. The other half is that the people in Sodom who were righteous failed at being salt in that society. They failed to shake the preserving influence of God's righteousness over Sodom's evil culture. In fact, the only reasons we know Lot was righteous is that he was spared from Sodom's judgment and that the Bible calls him "righteous Lot" (2 Peter 2:7). Lot is a real parable of the danger we face as believers today. He had made his peace with Sodom's sin and was enjoying its affluence to the point that he was having zero impact for righteousness. The Bible is clear that God sometimes blesses His people in spite of themselves, but that doesn't let them off the hook when it comes to living in obedience to Him. There's nothing wrong with having things, but when those things keep you from living for Christ, either you have too many things or your things have you. Don't let your blessings become a curse by leading you away from God.

Lot's "tasteless" life became painfully apparent when it came time for Sodom to be judged. Lot probably didn't know about God's agreement with Abraham to spare the city for ten righteous people, but it didn't matter, because he fell well short of the quota anyway. He couldn't even persuade his sons-in-law to come with him. It came down to Lot, his wife, and their two daughters. If Lot had impacted his extended family for God, that would have been six people, and if each one of these had influenced just one other person, Abraham would have had his ten righteous people with two to spare. But a righteous minority was nowhere to be found.

Salt's Thirst-Inducing Nature

Besides its preserving qualities, salt also creates thirst. As believers gather together in the name of Jesus Christ, the church's impact should not only have a preserving influence against the decay of evil, but the quality of our lives should also make people so thirsty for what we have that they are drawn to Christ like a parched man to water.

I was at an airport one day with some time to spare before my flight boarded, so I went to a little lounge area and ordered a soft drink. The waitress brought me my drink, but she also brought something else I didn't order: a bowl of salty peanuts that were on the house.

Now you know she didn't do that because the establishment simply wanted to thank me for my business, or because they wanted to enhance my airport experience so I would come back. The only purpose for that salty snack was to dry out my mouth and make me so thirsty that I would open my wallet and say, "Hit me again, Sam."

The job of the church is to create a thirst in the culture that can only be satisfied by the living water of Jesus Christ. We don't have to worry about trying to make Christianity attractive or palatable or relevant to the world. All we have to do is make people thirsty for Jesus. And don't forget that when lost people feel their thirst, they will be looking for a thirst-quencher. When Jesus offered the woman at the well a water that would quench her thirst forever, her response was, "Sir, give me this water, so I will not be thirsty" (John 4:15).

Let me ask you a question. Is there anyone at work, at school, or in the neighborhood who has become thirsty because your life is so salty for Christ? Or have you become tasteless salt that is so mixed with impurities the world is walking right over you? If you don't like the answer you come up with, now is the time to do something about it.

THE LIGHT OF THE WORLD

Jesus used a second familiar metaphor in Matthew 5 when He said of His people, "You are the light of the world. A city set on a hill cannot be hidden; nor does anyone light a lamp and put it under a basket, but on the lampstand, and it gives light to all who are in the house" (vv. 14–15).

Driving Back the Darkness

The last time I checked, the role of light was to shine, and in so doing to drive back the darkness. The world needs light because it sits in spiritual darkness. We were saved out of that darkness, and now our job is to shine the light of Christ back on the world's darkness. Paul told the Ephesians, "You were formerly darkness, but now you are Light in the Lord; walk as children of Light" (Ephesians 5:8).

When we are walking through this world as children of light, the world has a better chance to see things as they really are. "All things become visible when they are exposed by the light, for everything that becomes visible is light" (Ephesians 5:13). You know how hard it is to sleep when someone comes in and turns the light on in your face. That's the effect we should have on unbelievers who are sleeping the sleep of eternal death (see v. 14 of this same passage).

If you're in a dark room where people are groping for light and you know where the light switch is, it's a waste of time to organize a panel discussion on the effects of darkness or shake your head over how terrible the darkness is. Your assignment is to turn on the light, and the darkness will automatically be overcome.

Jesus went on to say, "Let your light shine before men" (Matthew 5:16a). In other words, carry your light out where it's dark so that unsaved people can see it. It would be ridiculous to turn on a lamp and then put something over it to hide its glow. If you say you want your house to be a welcoming place on a dark night, it would be foolish to turn the lights on and then close all the curtains so no one can tell you're home.

Yet, all too often, that's what we do in the church. Our lights burn brightly inside the church, but we are the only ones benefiting from them. Meanwhile, the world outside goes on in its darkness. But lights are designed to be displayed, not hidden. It's impossible to hide a light that's "set on a hill," and the farther the beam reaches, the more people who are affected by it. A local church that wants to measure its effectiveness only has to look into its community to see how far its light is penetrating the darkness.

Reflecting God's Glory

Don't misunderstand. We are not the light, but simply the reflector of Christ's light. It's interesting that before Satan fell into pride and rebelled against God, he was Lucifer, "the shining one" or "light-bearer." He is called "star of the morning" and "son of the dawn" in Scripture (Isaiah 14:12). As the highest-ranking angel, Lucifer's job was to reflect God's glory by leading heaven's worship. But Lucifer decided he wanted to *become* the light instead of just reflecting it, and God cast him out of heaven into darkness. Satan has been the prince of darkness ever since, and he's still trying to put out the light of God's glory. But God has set the church in the world as a "city on a hill" to reflect His glory.

Doing Good Works

This is what Jesus said in Matthew 5:16. The full verse says, "Let your light shine before men in such a way that they may see your good works, and glorify your Father who is in heaven." We need to talk about the concept of good works. Jesus not only mentioned them here, but Paul said of us, "For we are His workmanship, created in Christ Jesus for good works, which God prepared beforehand so that we would walk in them" (Ephesians 2:10). God also wants us to be "equipped for every good work" (2 Timothy 3:17).

So what are the good works Christians are called to do? They are the visible demonstration of Christ's love and power within us. Good works are the deeds of kindness and blessing that we do to benefit others, in the name of God and for His glory. They are important for the same reason that no one wants a television with sound only. People want a picture to go with the sound. People don't just want to hear us talk about God. They want to see actions that back up our faith.

It's true that unbelievers can do good things. They can build hospitals and orphanages and feed hungry people. But, by definition, the good things that non-Christians do are not done in God's name and therefore the motive is not to bring Him glory, even if there is a religious motivation behind the act.

The good works that we're talking about are based on God's Word and are done to give Him the credit, to shine the light on His glorious person. They are also to be done with surpassing excellence, which doesn't mean just bigger and better. Paul said, "[This] one thing I do" (Philippians 3:13), not "These ten things I dabble in." Everything we do, from our preaching and worship to our service to the community, should bear the stamp of God's character and be worthy of His name.

Our church in Dallas has a program that we call Project Turn Around to help take our witness for Christ into the community where it is needed. Through this program we go into more than fifty high schools to work with the students. We go to apartment complexes to reach out to people who are down and out. We help people get an education and acquire job skills, then help them find jobs and get homes. We develop businesses and provide medical assistance.

Why do we do this? Because the church is to be known for good works that benefit others so that people will be drawn to Christ. We are to put God on display, to advertise and show Him off. That's what it means to bring Him glory. When we do good works as the corporate body of Christ in His name and for His glory, we are calling attention to our awesome God and His all-encompassing kingdom.

BRINGING JUBILEE TO THE CULTURE

You see, people often don't understand that the gospel has two aspects. It has *content,* which is the message of faith alone in Christ alone for the forgiveness of sins and the gift of eternal life. The gospel's content is vertical, involving a person's relationship with God.

But the gospel also has horizontal *scope,* or effect, upon the world. The church should be "Ground Zero" where the gospel detonates, so to speak, and impacts everything and everyone around it in an ever-widening circle. Jesus addressed this aspect of the gospel in Luke 4, when He came back to His hometown of Nazareth one

Sabbath. He went into the synagogue and read from the scroll of Isaiah: "The Spirit of the Lord is upon Me, because He anointed Me to preach the gospel to the poor. He has sent Me to proclaim release to the captives, and recovery of sight to the blind, to set free those who are oppressed" (v. 18). Jesus said He came to proclaim liberty and freedom, to announce God's blessing being dispensed through what He called "the favorable year of the Lord" (v. 19).

This was the Old Testament Year of Jubilee, a special year observed every fifty years in which God set society back in order. During Jubilee slaves were released, debts were canceled, and land that had been sold reverted back to its original owner. Imagine what this did to achieve justice and bring blessing to Israeli society. If you were poor, Jubilee was good news because your debts were canceled. If you were in servitude to someone, you were set free at Jubilee.

Atonement Before Jubilee

But there's something else I want you to see. According to Leviticus 25:8–10, Israel could not have Jubilee until the people first observed the Day of Atonement. In other words, there could not be true blessing on the horizontal, human level until they got right with God on the vertical level. As long as people were not right with God, they could not enjoy the good news of Jubilee. You can't have jubilee without atonement.

Jesus Christ came to the Jews of His day and announced, "Repent, for the kingdom of heaven is at hand" (Matthew 4:17). In other words, "I am your Messiah. Receive Me as the Lamb of God, who will be slain for the atonement of your sins, and then I will bring you Jubilee, the kingdom of God." But when the people rejected atonement, they lost Jubilee.

Why is the church the key to the well-being of a community? Because we bring atonement, and what we say by our presence in the atonement is that this community can have Jubilee because atonement has been made. We are a forgiven people.

But we can never get the order reversed. The so-called social gospel tries to bring freedom from oppression and relief to the needy, which is the blessing of Jubilee, while ignoring the absolute necessity of atonement for sin. Jesus said our good works should point people to God and His glory, not become a substitute for God. My goal as a pastor is not to see how many people we can seat in our sanctuary, but to see how much of our community we can transform with the people God brings into our sanctuary.

Help or Take Down the Sign

The story is told of a young couple who got married and set out on their honeymoon. They were driving on a dark road that night when the car swerved off the road and crashed in a ditch. The groom awoke from the accident to find his beloved bride bleeding and unconscious. In desperation he gathered her into his arms and began looking around frantically for help.

Suddenly the young man looked up and saw a light shining from the porch of a house on the hill. Knowing that his bride wouldn't live long in her condition, he carried her up the hill to the house. As he came close to the house he got very excited, because there was a sign hanging on the porch that said, "John Smith, M.D."

The young groom rushed to the door and began knocking excitedly. An elderly gentleman came to the door, looked out into the darkness, and asked, "May I help you?"

"Sir," the groom cried out, "my bride has been hurt in an accident and is dying! Please save her!"

But the old man drew back and said, "I'm sorry, but I can't help you. I stopped practicing medicine twenty years ago."

The desperate groom looked at the old man in stunned anger and said, "Mister, your sign says you're a doctor. Either help my bride right now or take down that sign!"

The church either needs to impact its community for Christ, or take down our sign that advertises that a real church meets here. Being salt and light means that we have something life-changing to offer people in a decaying and dark world.

THE FUNCTION OF THE CHURCH

11

THE
LEADERSHIP
OF THE
CHURCH

Several years ago, a magazine for church leaders published a small cartoon that anyone involved in church ministry could readily identify with. The picture showed a pastor on his knees in his study, looking up with a startled expression his face. His secretary or some other church staff member is standing at the open door, having obviously just burst into the study, no doubt with some item that someone thought needed the pastor's immediate attention. The woman has a delighted look on her face, and the caption says, "Oh good. You're not busy!"

That little scenario has a valid point to make, because it is too often the case that instead of having adequate time to seek God for His vision and to study His Word, a pastor has to spend his time on matters that could and should be handled by someone else.

There are several reasons this happens. One is that some pastors feel they have to be part of every decision made in the church, no matter how trivial. That's a recipe for dissatisfaction by the people and burnout by the leader. Other churches don't have a proper leadership structure in place that allows for authority to be delegated to spiritually capable people so that the church moves forward without wearing out the pastor. In still other churches, the people's expectations of their leaders are not biblically grounded, so they bring all the church's work to the leaders' doors and leave it there.

A church may have one or more of these problems, and when this happens it's a serious issue. What I want you to see is that the Bible has clear principles and guidelines for leadership in the church. We need to know these so that the church is functioning biblically, leaders are being identified and developed as God intended, the body of Christ is being served, and the church is being equipped to take its ministry out into the streets where lives need to be changed.

A good working definition of leadership is to know the right way to go, to go that way yourself, and then to show the way for others. Leaders are people who know the way, go the way, and show the way. Leadership also implies "followership." If you call yourself a leader and nobody is following you, you are on a lonely walk. A shepherd who has no sheep is not really a shepherd.

There is another element we need to add to our definition of leadership, because spiritual leadership is different from secular leadership. Jesus articulated this further element when He said, "Even the Son of Man did not come to be served, but to serve" (Mark 10:45). Spiritual leaders are servant-leaders, setting the example by loving service rather than by cracking the whip and barking out orders to the rank-and-file.

Leadership is critical to the church because God's people need leaders who can stand before the church and say, "Thus saith the Lord." We call this process expository preaching, which is expounding the Word of God in such a way that His people understand it and know how to apply it. This is the pastor's primary calling as the shepherd of God's flock.

Biblically informed leadership is also necessary due to the limitation of human resources. One person only has so much time and energy. When there is ministry to be done or people who are hurting and need help, these things can't wait for months until the pastor can get to them. The Bible teaches the principle of delegation to help leaders meet the needs of God's people.

A third reason that leadership is important is that people do have needs and problems. Any pastor can tell you that folk don't leave their struggles and messes at home when they join the church. They drag all that stuff with them into the family, and things can become very complex.

But despite all of these challenges, God has a will for His people and a direction He wants them to move in. Church leadership is designed to guide God's people toward their divinely ordained objectives. Leadership involves both instruction and modeling, teaching people what God expects and then showing them by example how to achieve it.

A MODEL FOR CHURCH LEADERSHIP

With a basic definition of leadership in place, we need to see what is involved in the leadership of the New Testament church. But this issue doesn't really begin in the New Testament, because the basic paradigm or model for church leadership was established in Exodus 18, long before the church came into existence. And the idea for this model did not come from Israel's leaders, but from a man named Jethro, a priest from North Africa who was the father-in-law of Moses. It's important for us to spend some time on this story, because out of it comes the key principle that governs church leadership.

An Impossible Assignment

The situation in Exodus 18 was that Moses was trying to act as the "pastor" to a congregation of more than two million people. His father-in-law Jethro came to visit Moses (see vv. 1–13), watched him trying to deal with the people all by himself, and offered some wise advice:

> Now when Moses' father-in-law saw all that he was doing for the people, he said, "What is this thing that you are doing for the people? Why do you alone sit as judge and all the people stand about you from morning until evening?" Moses said to his father-in-law, "Because the people come to me to inquire of God. When they have a dispute, it comes to me, and I judge between a man and his neighbor and make known the statutes of God and His laws." (vv. 14–16)

Moses was getting up every morning at dawn and staying up until dark, trying to render decisions for a long line of people. They streamed to him with their problems, and woe be to anyone who needed a follow-up session or further counseling. They were in for a long wait.

How did Moses get into this mess? I believe the Bible gives us the answer as we review what had happened to the Israelites in the desert up to this point. For example, Exodus 14 contains the thrilling story of Israel's deliverance at the Red Sea. The people were trapped with the sea blocking their route, and Pharaoh and his Egyptian army were coming after them. So the Israelites got scared and cried out to Moses, "Is it because there were no graves in Egypt that you have taken us away to die in the wilderness? Why have you dealt with us in this way, bringing us out of Egypt?" (v. 11).

The people were saying to Moses, "If it weren't for you and your leadership, we wouldn't be in this mess. You're going to be the death of us out here."

But God told Moses to stretch out his staff over the Red Sea and part it so the people could pass over safely, while the Egyptians were drowned. After this deliverance, the Bible says that the people "believed in the Lord and in His servant Moses" (v. 31). The people were saying to Moses, "Mo, you are our man! Do we have a great leader or what! You lead and we will follow." So things turned around for Moses, but not for long.

Just three days later (Exodus 15:22), the people were thirsty. When they came to Marah and found they could not drink the water, they began to gripe at Moses again, "We want a drink of water!" (see v. 24). So Moses prayed, and God gave him the solution to the problem (v. 25). But the problems still weren't over for Moses, because after they got water the people got hungry and started griping again (Exodus 16:2). This time they brought the "assistant pastor" into it, griping against Aaron too. You know it's bad when people complain against the assistant pastor!

This time the people even accused Moses of trying to kill them: "Would that we had died by the Lord's hand in the land of Egypt, when we sat by the pots of meat, when we ate bread to the full; for you have brought us out into this wilderness to kill this whole assembly with hunger" (Exodus 16:3).

These folk were sitting around saying, "Boy, that was some good home cooking we had back there in Egypt. Sure do miss that fried chicken and mama's homemade bread." The people accused Moses of not caring about them, so God provided another miraculous provision with quail and manna, corn flakes from heaven (vv. 13–21). The people had all they wanted to eat.

But things soon turned ugly again when the congregation got upset with Moses because they were thirsty. This time, however, the people hit Mo with a low blow. They not only accused him of trying to kill them, but their animals and even their children (see Exodus 17:3).

So here's the picture. Ever since they left Egypt, the Israelites have been charging Moses with not caring about them. So Moses was wearing himself out trying to act as pastor, judge, and counselor because he was trying to show the people that he did care. And this was one way he could prove his concern for them.

Wearing Out the Pastor

This brings us back to Exodus 18 and Moses' impossible task of trying to lead Israel by himself. Jethro watched Moses knock himself out, and then gave him this counsel: "The thing that you are doing is not good. You will surely wear out, both yourself and these people who are with you, for the task is too heavy for you; you cannot do it alone" (vv. 17–18).

The Hebrew words *wear out* mean to fade away. Moses was going to put himself in the grave trying to deal with all these problems, and the people were going to suffer too. Jethro was saying, "Moses, people who are in conflict and crisis can't wait a month or two for your schedule to open up."

This, unfortunately, is the case with too many pastors. Some poor pastor wears himself out trying to do everything and see everybody, and then the people stand at his funeral and say, "Oh, wasn't he a good pastor? He was down there at the church from dawn to dusk every day. He did everything for us. We sure are going to miss him."

That's not the way the ministry is supposed to work. Moses was wearing himself out dealing with all the problems, but even more important, he didn't have time to accomplish his primary ministry, which was to go before God, get His word, and then teach it to the people. So Jethro told Moses:

> Now listen to me: I will give you counsel, and God be with you. You be the people's representative before God, and you bring the disputes to God, then teach them the statutes and the laws, and make known to them the way in which they are to walk and the work they are to do. (vv. 19–20)

The Principle of Representation

Jethro told Moses to bring the people's disputes before God, get God's answers for those problems, and then communicate God's Word to the people in such a way that they would know how to apply God's truth to their lives. Today in the church this is expository preaching, which we talked about earlier as a pastor's primary calling and responsibility.

When a pastor goes before God to seek His Word and His will

for the people, he is serving as a representative. This is the role that Jethro counseled Moses to take in the verses quoted above. Representation is a fundamental principle of Scripture that is often overlooked when we talk about the church, but it is crucial to understand if we are going to do church God's way.

The principle of representation permeates Scripture. For example, all of us are born spiritually dead in Adam because when Adam sinned in the Garden of Eden, he was functioning as the representative head of the human race. Therefore, Adam's sin was transferred to all of his children through his representation, and spiritual death passed on to all of us because we have all sinned.

The good news is that if you are a Christian, you have changed representatives. Instead of being in Adam, you are now in Christ. I love the way Paul stated it: "For as in Adam all die, so also in Christ all will be made alive" (1 Corinthians 15:22). And Jesus' representation on our behalf extends into the courtroom of heaven, for according to 1 John 2:1 He is our "advocate," or defense attorney, before the Father in heaven. He is there pleading our case, which is great for us because that means our Attorney is related to the Judge.

The principle of representation came into play again a few chapters after Exodus 18 when Moses was on the mountain receiving the Ten Commandments and the people persuaded Aaron to make the golden calf (see Exodus 32:1–6). God's anger was so fierce against Israel that He told Moses He was going to destroy those rebels and start over with Moses. Verses 8–14 describe this conversation between God and Moses, in which Moses went before God and said, "Lord, You can't do this. First, You would be breaking Your promises to Israel. And second, Your great name will be dishonored among the nations who will say You were strong enough to deliver Your people from Egypt, but not strong enough to lead them to the Promised Land." The Bible says that God changed His mind about destroying Israel because Moses stood in the gap as the people's representative.

Out nation operates by the representative system of government. The president and the Congress can take actions and lead us into a war that we may not agree with because they are our representatives. You'll remember that "No taxation without representation" was a rallying cry of the American colonies that helped lead to the Revolutionary War.

Jethro's advice to Moses drew on this great principle of representation. Moses was in a mediatorial position between God and the people, the same position a husband is to take in his home and the pastor is to take in the church. Biblical church leadership is impossible without God's representatives.

Delegating to Godly Leaders

In Exodus 18:21–23, we read of Jethro's further counsel to Moses. This involved selecting men of good character and spiritual integrity to help Moses in administering justice and meeting needs among the Israelites. The organization was classic, with "leaders of thousands, of hundreds, of fifties and of tens" (v. 21). Thus Moses developed a system whereby the people could get to a leader quickly when they had a need. These leaders would "judge the people at all times" (v. 22), and there was a chain of command established so that only the hardest cases had to be forwarded up the line to Moses.

This was the foundation of the later system of elders who ruled in each Israeli community. The rulers Moses appointed were to oversee the application of God's truth to the people as He revealed it to Moses. Remember that Moses' job was to go before God and get His Word for the people, then teach it to them. The leaders had to know the truth, which means that Moses had to work with these men to train them and develop them for their roles.

This is critical to the functioning of the church today because the basic principle is the same. A pastor should be spending time with his leaders instilling God's Word in their hearts. The church doesn't need leaders primarily to administer budgets, although that is part of leadership. The church needs leaders who can provide biblical answers and effective ministry to the needs and challenges that the people face.

Every month I get together with all of our church leaders for two hours. All I do the first hour is teach the Word. We have a leaders' notebook that provides them with the outlines of what I'm teaching so they can be ready to give an answer on various issues to the people under their leadership. That way we are all on the same page when it comes to the church's answer on things such as divorce or other issues that may arise.

The selection of the seven deacons in the church at Jerusalem provides an early example of church leadership principles at work (see Acts 6:1–7). There was a legitimate need that had to be addressed, the neglect of the Hellenistic or Greek widows in the daily administration of food. The apostles said it was not right for them to leave their primary calling as the people's representatives before God to address this need, so they directed the church to put forward spiritual men who could administer this task.

All of the deacons selected in Acts 6 had Greek names, which means the church chose these men sensitively and strategically, since it was Greek widows who were hurting. The need was met, and the church enjoyed peace and continued to grow. When people have needs, they need someone in the church who can respond to them.

In the case of Moses, Jethro mentioned three important benefits that would come from Moses' appointment of leaders for the people. Jethro told Moses, "It will be easier for you, and they will bear the burden with you" (Exodus 18:22). Then he added, "You will be able to endure, and all these people also will go to their place in peace" (v. 23). Proper leadership will enable a pastor to minister longer because he is not bearing the load alone. When I teach other pastors I often tell them that Jesus has already died for their people, so they don't need to die for them too. The people of God already have a Savior who is perfectly sufficient, so the pastor doesn't need to try to fill that role.

Moses was still available to handle the tough cases that could not be solved at the lower echelons of leadership. The New Testament makes a similar provision for the church in the church court, described in 1 Corinthians 6:1–8. The church should have its own system to settle issues and resolve disputes between believers, and the people should take the church's decisions as binding.

We have a court in our church that meets every week. Our elders sit on the court to hear and decide the cases, and we take this very seriously because the Bible says it is to the church's "shame" when believers take their disputes to the unrighteous (vv. 5–6). We arbitrate cases in our church court because we believe that this is part of operating biblically. Why should the church adjudicate its own matters? Because God has His own set of rules that are different than the rules of this world order.

THE LEVELS OF CHURCH LEADERSHIP

This is a long background to bring us to the New Testament's teaching on the church's leadership, but it is important to establish the principles upon which this leadership is based. With this backdrop we are ready to look at the church's leaders and their qualifications. The Bible identifies three distinct leadership roles for the church, which are pastor, elder, and deacon.

The Office of Pastor

The pastor, or pastor-teacher as described by Paul in Ephesians 4:11, is the church's spiritual leader. In a multiple staff church, the senior pastor is charged with the primary responsibility for the church's spiritual health and direction. I would summarize the pastor's role as proclaiming the Word and overseeing the work, which includes developing leaders who are qualified to serve as elders and deacons.

Make no mistake about it. No matter how big a church's staff may be, there is always a primary leader who has been invested by God with authority and responsibility. This leader is not a despot, and he is accountable to the body of elders (see 1 Timothy 5:17 NIV, where the elders are said to "direct the affairs of the church"). The church's leadership does not rest in committees. There has to be a place where "the buck stops," and there has to be a leader who leads the way in formulating and implementing the church's vision. God always transfers leadership to a person, whether it be from Moses to Joshua, Elijah to Elisha, or Paul to Timothy. God places His vision in the hands of a person.

The Office of Elder

The second New Testament classification of leaders is the elders—which are always talked about in the plural, by the way. These are the spiritually qualified men who form the governing body of the church and in whose hands the final policy decisions rest. (The pastor is an elder also, for Paul talked about elders "who work hard at preaching and teaching," 1 Timothy 5:17.)

I do not believe the Bible teaches congregational rule. The Bible clearly teaches congregational involvement, but not congregational government in which the church body at large has the final authority. Why is this? Because you don't want to have carnal people voting on the will of God. There is this assumption in the church that if we put a matter before the people, they will have the spiritual insight and biblical knowledge to make a right decision. Now this may be the case with some of the people, but God's will has never been subject to majority vote.

Do you know why the children of Israel never got to the Promised Land when they should have? Because they took a congregational vote and the majority prevailed. Ten spies said they couldn't conquer the land, and two spies said they could. The congregation voted with the ten, and the nation turned back into the desert. The selection of the first deacons in Acts 6 was the result of congregational involvement in putting these men before the apostles. But the apostles made the final decision by approving the men and laying hands on them to set them apart for their task.

The Bible also teaches that elders must be men. "If any man aspires to the office of overseer, it is a fine work he desires to do" (1 Timothy 3:1). The word for *man* is the gender specific word for males. The principle of male leadership in the church is established earlier in 1 Timothy: "I do not allow a woman to teach or exercise authority over a man" (2:12). Paul's statement in 1 Corinthians 14:34–35 that women are to be silent in church doesn't mean they can't speak. The issue there is authority.

Let me add that I am not talking about spiritual gifts here, but the *office* of elder. Women in the church are very gifted, even more so than men in many cases. And God allows women to use their gifts in the church. In fact, I believe women can do anything in church except be an elder or a pastor. But final leadership in the church is restricted to men.

The clear pattern in Scripture is a plurality of elders in each church. For example, Acts 14:23 says that Paul and his missionary team appointed "elders [plural] for them in every church [singular]." James tells us that if anyone is sick, he should "call for the elders of the church" (James 5:14), the same pattern as in Acts. Paul left Titus in Crete to "appoint elders in every city" (Titus 1:5). Timothy's spiritual gift was bestowed by "the presbytery," or the governing board of the church at Ephesus (1 Timothy 4:14).

The plurality of elders solves the problem of who is in charge and who has the final authority in the church. There is often a lot of jockeying for power, but I believe the answer to the problem is fairly simple. The board of elders establishes the policies that govern the church's ministry, in line with Scripture. The pastor works within these guidelines and is accountable to the elders, with the freedom to set the church's vision and ministry direction.

An analogy that may help is to liken the elders' ministry to setting the boundaries for a football game. The pastor is like the quarterback, who is free to call the plays and move the team down the field under his leadership, as long as he stays within the boundaries. But if the pastor steps out-of-bounds, the elders blow the whistle and deal with the infraction. The goal is authority with accountability, but without unnecessary restriction.

What happens if the rest of the team doesn't want to execute the plays the pastor calls? Then conflict is inevitable. That's why it is so important for the pastor, the elders, and the deacons to be of the same spirit. God told Moses to choose seventy elders, concerning whom God said, "I will take of the Spirit who is upon you, and will put Him upon them" (Numbers 11:17). The pastor's heartbeat needs to be the other leaders' heartbeat. There is no room in a church for competing visions if it is to function biblically.

The Office of Deacon

The Greek word for deacon means "servant." This office is interesting because nowhere in Scripture do we find a deacon board. There is the presbytery, or elder board, but no corresponding formal organization of deacons. This is because the deacons only have one basic job, which is to execute the church policies and ministries that have been established by the elders and the pastor.

Deacons are to do more than serve communion and count the offerings. They must be spiritually mature and responsible men and women. Yes, I believe women can be deacons because of 1 Timothy 3:11, which says, "Women must likewise be dignified, not malicious gossips, but temperate, faithful in all things." In the context Paul is talking about women who serve as deacons, since he mentions deacons' wives in verse 12.

Paul used the word *women* here because there is no Greek word for "deaconess." These women are clearly distinguished from deacons' wives. He was not saying that only men can be deacons, but that those men who are selected be faithful to their wives. If verse 11 is only talking about deacons' wives, we have a problem because that means Paul skipped over the qualifications for elders' wives. This would have made deacons' wives more important and under closer scrutiny than the wives of elders. So it is clear to me that Paul was talking about deaconesses, or women who function on an equal level with male deacons. Paul called Phoebe "a servant," the same word for deacon (Romans 16:1).

The job of deacons is to fan out among the flock to make sure that the ministry gets done. They are the church's foot soldiers. Every one of the more than 135 ministries in our church is headed by a deacon or deaconness. This puts them in touch with the people to stimulate their involvement and meet their needs. Deacons are accountable to the elders, but the biblical pattern indicates that deacons do not come together as a separate governing board.

THE QUALIFICATIONS
OF CHURCH LEADERS

One thing is clear concerning the qualifications of church leaders. The lists in 1 Timothy 3:1–13 and Titus 1:6–9 deal first and foremost with character and the pursuit of a godly lifestyle on the part of those who aspire to lead in the body of Christ. Having skilled but carnal people doesn't help the church. Neither is it helped by people who have their own agenda to push.

There are well over a dozen qualifications for elders and deacons mentioned in 1 Timothy 3, some of which are repeated in the qualifications for elders outlined in Titus 1. You can read and compare these lists in detail for yourself, but what I want to do here is combine the lists and review the major categories of qualifications to give you a sense of the kind of people God considers qualified to lead His people. I won't try to give chapter and verse for each individual item, but will mention selected verses to keep us oriented to the text.

It's worth noting again that a potential elder should "aspire" to this office (1 Timothy 3:1). This doesn't mean he should campaign for the job, but he should be willing to serve if asked. The church should not be pressuring reluctant candidates into leadership positions just because there are vacancies to fill. That's a recipe for problems and a pastoral headache.

In terms of their qualifications, both elders and deacons must be temperate or self-controlled. This quality not only means freedom from excess in their personal habits, but also in their attitude toward things such as money. The other side of this coin is prudence, or a well-ordered life. The goal is a person whose personal and family life is solid, showing depth of character and the ability to manage a family and a household well. The need for these qualities is obvious. "If a man does not know how to manage his own household, how will he take care of the church of God?" (1 Timothy 3:5).

Paul used a number of terms to refer to the fact that elders and deacons also need to be people of even temperament. They cannot have a violent temper or be "pugnacious," the kind of people who are always ready for an argument or a fight and pound their fists on the table when things don't go their way. I heard of a pastor who ran into a cantankerous board member at church one Sunday. "I'm sorry I missed the board meeting last week," the man told the pastor. "I was looking forward to voting no."

Too many pastors can identify with this brother's problem. Some church leaders may think God called them to be the monkey wrench in the works, but that's not the picture the Bible gives. "Troublemaker" or "naysayer" is not a church job description. A person who is habitually angry, disagreeable, and harsh-spirited rather than gentle and peaceable is not biblically qualified to lead in the church.

Church leaders must also have good reputations. Nobody is perfect, but "above reproach" (1 Timothy 3:2) means that no one can lay a charge of improper behavior against them. The other side of this is the quality of hospitality and unselfish generosity, someone whose home and heart is open to others. Being above reproach also means a leader who is just and impartial in his decisions, not allowing himself to be swayed by the opinions of others.

An elder must also be "able to teach" and "not a new convert" (1 Timothy 3:2, 6), meaning that he must have a track record of demonstrated spiritual maturity, commitment to the truth of Scripture, and an ability to handle the Word. These qualifications reflect the teaching office of elders, a qualification that is not repeated for deacons because they are in a different role. Deacons can teach, of course, but it is the elders who are responsible for what is taught in the church.

The family life of elders and deacons is very important, since the way they lead their families is a reliable indicator of the way they will lead in the church. Elders and male deacons need to be faithful

husbands, literally "a one-woman man." The reference to the conduct of a leader's children doesn't mean there are never any problems in the home. It may even be that an elder or a deacon must deal
with a rebellious child. The issue isn't the problem itself, but the way
the leader handles it. As a pastor, I want to see leaders who manage their families and deal with problems head-on instead of letting the problems manage them.

One other area of qualifications deals with the honesty and
integrity of leaders. We mentioned earlier the need for church leaders to be free from greed and honest in their financial dealings. They
must also "lov[e] what is good" (Titus 1:8). This means pursuing the
best things in life, not the sordid or questionable. It's great to know
that a potential elder is not tangled up in pornography, for example. But is he also a faithful student of the Word who fills his mind
with what is good (see Philippians 4:8) instead of the stuff that comes
into his home through the popular media? God wants His leaders to
be able to stand up to the scrutiny of the church and have a good
reputation with the unbelieving world.

KEEPING THE STANDARD HIGH

There has been a popular idea floating around for a long time
that the church needs to function like a business, with the same basic
structure. That's why it is often assumed that the best people to
lead the church are leaders in the business community. So we look
for corporate CEOs to chair the church's board and accountants to
do the church's books.

There is certainly nothing wrong with tapping business leaders
to serve in the church, if they are spiritually qualified. And the church
needs to conduct its financial affairs in an orderly way with integrity.
But I do not believe that we need a business manual to operate the
church. The secular world should not be telling us how to govern a
spiritual institution. God has told the church in His Word how to
conduct His work, so why should we take our cues from the world?
As we said earlier, the church operates by a different standard.

The church's distinctiveness is underscored in the verses that follow the list of leader qualifications in 1 Timothy 3:1–13. You'll recognize verses 14–16 as a text we studied thoroughly in an earlier chapter. I just want to point this passage out again so you can see these verses in their context.

The leaders God wants must be distinct in their qualifications because the church is not just any organization. It is God's "household" (v. 15), or family, made up of people who are related to God and to each other. And in God's house, His rules are in force.

It's also important to have the right leaders because the church is "the pillar and support of the truth" (v. 15). You'll remember that Paul was alluding to the many pillars supporting the temple of Artemis in Ephesus. These pillars were upholding a lie, but the church and only the church is charged with upholding the truth.

What does this mean for the church's ministry? It means that the church must never lower its standard to accommodate the world. Don't get me wrong. The church must minister to people who are not operating by God's standards. But the goal is to elevate the people, not lower the standard so everyone can get in easily. Too many churches today have lowered the standard of truth to "relate" to people and make them feel more comfortable. But all that does is give people a false sense of well-being.

This reminds me of an incident that happened when my son Jonathan was about nine or ten years old. He is playing football at Baylor University as I write this, but in those days his game was basketball. Jonathan came running to me one day and said, "Daddy, I can dunk a basketball!"

He was only about five feet tall at the time, so I was skeptical. But he wanted to show me that he could dunk, so I followed him over to the church's gym. There I found out that the janitor had lowered the basketball goal so Jonathan could reach it. He excitedly showed me how he could dunk the ball with two hands.

I've said before that the reason God gives preachers families is for sermon illustrations. Well, I saw a chance for a real-life illustration. So after I applauded my son's effort, I asked the janitor to raise the goal back up to its true standard of ten feet. Then I said to Jonathan, "Son, what you did is fine. But I just want you to know that this is where you want to be someday."

I didn't want Jonathan to miss the point that his lowering of the standard didn't change the rules of basketball. When the church lowers its standard of biblical truth to accommodate people, we are simply making them feel good about wrong things. The church needs to hold to the truth of God, and there is no better way to do this than by making sure that our leaders are godly people who are "holding fast the faithful word which is in accordance with the teaching, so that [they] will be able both to exhort in sound doctrine and refute those who contradict" (Titus 1:9).

12

THE UNITY OF THE CHURCH

A wonderful ceremony takes place each time an American athlete wins a gold medal in the Olympic Games. The athlete stands on a platform as the American flag is raised and a special song is played. Since America's Olympic athletes are representing their country and not themselves, they don't get to choose the song to be played while they're on the platform, nor can they say anything they want or wear any old outfit they feel like wearing. The song is the national anthem, the dress is the team's Olympic uniform, and the focus is as much on the athlete's nation as it is on the individual athlete.

The Olympic medal ceremony is a great reminder of the fact that these men and women are part of something much bigger than themselves. They are members of a community, united around the common goal of winning as many medals as possible to bring greater honor and glory to the nation they represent. When one athlete wins or loses, the whole community should rejoice or suffer together, because they are wearing the same uniform and pursuing the same goal.

Olympic unity doesn't function perfectly, because athletes are imperfect human beings. But their *function* doesn't change the *fact* that they are united under one banner. The same is true of the church. The fact is that God designed the church to be a unity of believers, whether we function that way or not. If you are a believer in Jesus Christ, He has a purpose for you here on earth that is much bigger than your individual salvation. You were born into a community of believers when God saved you, and He wants you to function within that community.

In our individualistic society it is easy to lose sight of the fact that Christians are bonded together in a relationship of unity with each other. God takes this relationship so seriously that the Bible warns us to watch out for people who cause division in the church, because they are harming Christ's body. And those who withdraw from the community of believers will find their relationship with God limited by their failure to participate in the fellowship of the saints.

A Christian who isn't interested in helping keep "the unity of the Spirit" (Ephesians 4:3) is like a child in a family who wants food, clothing, shelter, and all the privileges of family while refusing to help out around the house. Most families don't work that way, and neither does God's family, the church. The individual benefits come with corporate responsibility.

THE CONCEPT OF OUR UNITY

The Bible teaches that the unity of the church is the Holy Spirit's assignment and ministry. The Spirit extends this unity each time a person is saved, as Paul explained in 1 Corinthians 12: "For even as the body is one and yet has many members, and all the members of the body, though they are many, are one body, so also is Christ. For by one Spirit we were all baptized into one body, whether Jews or Greeks, whether slaves or free, and we were all made to drink of one Spirit" (vv. 12–13). Our spiritual unity as Christians is as organic as the unity of the human body.

The word *unity* means oneness, but that is different from sameness. Over the centuries the church has suffered from the misguided efforts of those who try to make everyone conform to their standards and keep their lists of dos and don'ts. But the unity of the Spirit does not deny our individual uniqueness as people made in God's image. It would be incredibly boring if God made us all alike.

God doesn't do that, which makes life in the body of Christ a lot more exciting and challenging. Unity in Christ is possible because we are united around Him—bowing to His Lordship and obeying His commands. True unity is finding oneness of purpose and commitment, moving toward a common goal, despite our differences. Unity doesn't require that we all be the same, but that we all head in the same direction.

Paul spent the rest of 1 Corinthians 12 showing how the church's unity functions in the midst of our differences (see vv. 14–31). His illustration of the human body reminds us that the body's various parts are designed to work together as a harmonious whole to accomplish the body's tasks. If you have ever broken your arm or leg and then tried to dress yourself, shower, and get around, you know how the body is weakened and hindered when one part isn't functioning properly.

Notice that Paul said, "The body is not one member, but many" (v. 14). That is a recognition of our individuality. But then he stopped in the middle of his discourse on the importance of each body part to give the other side of the coin: "Now there are many members, but one body" (v. 20). Both statements are true. We could liken the church to an intricate puzzle with hundreds or even thousands of pieces, no two of which are alike. But when the puzzle master has finished interlocking all the parts, the result is a complete picture.

A Big Job to Do

The fact that the church's unity is an organic reality wrought by the Holy Spirit doesn't mean it's easy to pull off. The problem isn't the Spirit's lack of power, of course, but the flawed human beings who make up Christ's body. There's no better example of this than the Spirit's work of bringing Jews and Gentiles together in the church.

The Jew-Gentile problem of the first century was the epitome of racial, religious, and cultural divisions. Jews wanted nothing to do with Gentiles. Gentiles were "dogs" to the Jews. The Gentiles didn't want to deal with the Jews either. The hostilities were real, and into the middle of this mess came the Holy Spirit.

We read earlier that the Spirit baptizes all believers into Christ's body, "whether Jews or Greeks." That statement doesn't register on our radar today, since comparatively few Jews come to Christ today and those who do rarely come to our Gentile churches. But in the early church, mentioning these two groups in the same sentence meant that something unusual was happening.

What was happening was that the Holy Spirit was blending Jews and Gentiles together into one body. The Bible says that this process involved having to overcome hostility and break down walls. It's worth quoting Paul's classic statement of what God did through Christ:

> Remember that formerly you, the Gentiles in the flesh, who are called "Uncircumcision" by the so-called "Circumcision" . . . remember that you were at that time separate from Christ, excluded from the commonwealth of Israel, and strangers to the covenants of promise, having no hope and without God in the world. But now in Christ Jesus you who formerly were far off have been brought near by the blood of Christ. For He Himself is our peace, who made both groups into one and broke down the barrier of the dividing wall, by abolishing in His flesh the enmity . . . thus establishing peace. (Ephesians 2:11–15)

The immensity of the task of uniting Jews and Gentiles into one harmonious body cannot be overstated. Jews believed that Gentiles could not enjoy God's favor, and even after the Spirit came at

Pentecost and the church was born, early Jewish believers expressed genuine surprise that God was saving Gentiles. As Peter preached to the Gentile household and friends of the Roman centurion Cornelius, the Holy Spirit fell on the people and the Jews with Peter were "amazed" (Acts 10:45). Later, when Peter was called to answer for his actions in going to Gentiles (a forbidden thing under the old rules), he explained that it was God's doing and quieted the objections (see Acts 11:18).

When the church came into being and the Holy Spirit began uniting a crowd of different people into one body, all of a sudden a person's religious standing, racial background, or social class was no longer preeminent. The early church not only contained Jews and Gentiles, but also slaves and slave owners, rich and poor people, the cultural and educational elite alongside folk from the "sticks."

But none of these old divisions mattered in the church—and, in fact, whenever those old divisions did start to matter the result was disunity and problems. Read Galatians 2:11–21 and recall the upset and hurt that Peter caused when he forsook his Gentile brothers in Antioch because some Jews from the 'hood in Jerusalem showed up. James 2 is a diatribe against the church for the shameful way they were treating poor people who came into the assembly. The Holy Spirit brings unity in the church. But when the Spirit is quenched through pride or prejudice, the result is disunity and a crippling of Christ's body.

You've heard the old saying that oil and water don't mix. That's true, unless something else is brought into the mix. One example is mayonnaise, which I like to put on my sandwiches. I'm glad someone found a way to make oil and water mix, because two of mayonnaise's ingredients are soybean oil and water. For the oil and water to mix they need an emulsifier, an ingredient that can reach out to the water and the oil and bind them together so that they don't go their own way. The emulsifying ingredient in mayonnaise is eggs, which grab the water and the oil and say to them, "You aren't going your own way, because we are going to make mayonnaise today."

When the Holy Spirit takes over, black people can get together with white people, and rich and poor people can treat each other as family. The Holy Spirit is the divine emulsifier, binding together people of different colors and personalities in the family of God. The Spirit's indispensable role in church unity is obvious from the opening verses of 1 Corinthians 12. Notice how many times Paul emphasized the unifying work of the Spirit amid the wide variety of gifts among believers: "the same Spirit" (vv. 4, 8, 9), "the one Spirit" (v. 9), and "one and the same Spirit" (v. 11).

And just so we know that the other two members of the Trinity are also committed to the church's unity, these verses talk about "the same Lord" (v. 5), who is Jesus Christ, and "the same God" (v. 6), a reference to God the Father. The Father, Son, and Holy Spirit are a perfect example of unity among distinct Persons with distinct functions, and the church is to reflect this same unity even though ours is far from perfect.

Jesus' Prayer for Unity

We've seen that the church's unity is a divine operation, coming down from above and working from within rather than being imposed from the outside. This is clear in Jesus' great high priestly prayer in the Upper Room the night before His crucifixion. The first discussion of the church's unity was not between Jews and Gentiles, or any other group of people. It was between the Father and the Son.

In the middle of His prayer, Jesus prayed on behalf of the people who believed in Him, "Holy Father, keep them in Your name, the name which You have given Me, that they may be one even as We are" (John 17:11). Then in verses 20–23 we read:

> I do not ask on behalf of these [the apostles] alone, but for those also who believe in Me through their word; that they may all be one; even as You, Father, are in Me and I in You, that they also may be in Us, so that the world may believe that You sent Me. The glory which You have given Me I have given to them, that they may be one, just as We are one; I in them and You in Me, that they may be perfected in unity, so

that the world may know that You sent Me, and loved them, even as You have loved Me.

This prayer shows how much is at stake in the church's unity. God's name, His glory, and His love are tied to the unity in which His people are to live. You see, our bond as believers in Christ is much more than something to keep us from fussing and fighting among ourselves. It is a testimony to the world that the Lord and the faith we preach are real.

There is no doubt that the Father answered the Son's prayer for unity, because God the Father and Jesus exist in complete unity. The only time the Father ever said no to a request from His beloved Son was when Jesus prayed that He might be spared the suffering of the cross. But even in that case, Jesus finished His prayer by saying, "Yet not what I will, but what You will" (Mark 14:36).

Now let me ask you a question. If God the Father responds to Jesus on the basis of their unity, how will God respond to us, since Jesus asked that we also be unified? The answer is that God will respond to us on the basis of our unity, or lack thereof.

Please don't misunderstand. Our relationship with God will never be the same as His relationship with Jesus, because we are not God. By using the term *relationship,* I am not talking about salvation. True believers can never lose their salvation. But the principle is what I'm getting at here. The church's unity is key to our blessing, service, and effectiveness for Christ, both corporately and individually.

Let me state this principle another way. If we are functioning in conflict and disunity rather than unity, God will limit His work in our lives. If we have time to be blessed but not be a blessing; if we are selfish saints who want things from God but don't want to mess with being a functioning member of a local church; or if we are causing disruption in the church by our attitudes or tongues, then we are wasting our time to get on our knees and ask God to do something for us. If we don't want to hang with His other children, what makes us think that our Daddy in heaven will support our rebellion?

There is a great example of this principle at work in the home.

In 1 Peter 3:7, the apostle told husbands who are in disunity with their wives to get their act together, "so that your prayers will not be hindered." That's another way of saying that a husband who is mistreating his wife and abusing their relationship need not bother having devotions, because God is not listening. God is saying, "If you are not fulfilling that which promotes unity in the home, we don't really have anything to talk about."

The Attack on Unity

Now if you were the devil and you knew that unity was the key to answered prayer and effectiveness among Christians, what would you do? You would sow disunity and cause a mess. You would create scenes in which people aren't talking or are glaring at each other out of the corner of their eyes. You would do everything possible to split believers apart, knowing that the power of God would be hindered.

Isn't that exactly what we are seeing today in the church? God's supernatural power is largely missing, in spite of all the resources and people we have. There are divisions of every kind, whether racial, cultural, social, attitudinal, or personal. But God won't work in the midst of conflict because He is perfect unity.

That's why the Bible says watch out for anybody in the church who causes disruption. "I urge you, brethren, keep your eye on those who cause dissensions and hindrances contrary to the teaching which you learned, and turn away from them" (Romans 16:17). Elsewhere Paul said concerning the church, "If any man destroys the temple of God, God will destroy him" (1 Corinthians 3:17). And among those things God hates is this: "One who spreads strife among brothers" (Proverbs 6:19). This is not a small issue, because God responds to His people's unity.

THE POWER OF OUR UNITY

It's not surprising that we find some amazing examples of the unified church in action in the book of Acts, which is after all the story of the church. Jesus had told the disciples not to go anywhere or do anything until the Holy Spirit came. So the apostles and the rest of the disciples went to an upper room in Jerusalem, where "these all with one mind were continually devoting themselves to prayer" (Acts 1:14). These disciples, who numbered 120, went into God's presence and called on Him as one person. They were all on the same page and heading in the same direction, and the Spirit came in power at Pentecost.

When this happened, three thousand people were saved in one day (see Acts 2:41). Verses 42–47 of Acts 2 are a portrait of a church united. These believers worshiped and fellowshipped together, and even shared their possessions with anyone in need. They were still of "one mind" (v. 46), and the results were powerful. There was "a sense of awe" and the apostles were performing many wonders (v. 43). And people were getting saved daily (see v. 47). God not only showed *up* in the church's midst, but He showed *out* to the people outside the assembly. Sometimes we forget that even though we must express our individual faith in Christ in order to get to heaven, it takes more than us by ourselves to get some heaven here on earth.

There is a huge difference between a laser and a spotlight. They are both beams of light, but the laser has far greater power because its photons of light are concentrated. The spotlight's photons are scattered, so that a laser can cut through steel while a spotlight can only illuminate the steel.

This is why the church's corporate unity and ministry are so important. When a body of people who are indwelt by the Holy Spirit gather in Christ's name to worship, pray, and serve with one mind and heart, the Spirit's power is concentrated like a laser—and things happen that we wouldn't see if the body was all split apart and disunified.

The early church understood the power of the corporate body. That's why when the apostles were threatened by the authorities, the Bible says that the church came together and "lifted their voices to God with one accord" (Acts 4:24). And when they were through, the building shook (see v. 31).

There's an even more dramatic account in Acts 12:3–19, Peter's imprisonment and deliverance. There is no record that Peter prayed for his own release, although he probably did. But we do know that "many were gathered together and were praying" for Peter (v. 12). And God sent an angel to bail the apostle out. This is the collective power of the church at work, and the key was their unity.

Some time ago a young woman in one of our church's families turned up missing. No one could find her, and a lot of people were praying. But one Wednesday night we brought the entire congregation together and prayed for this girl by name. The laser beam of God's power was concentrated on a need, and the next day she contacted her family, saying she felt compelled to call home.

THE FUNCTIONING OF OUR UNITY

The church's unity did not originate with us, but with God. It is the Holy Spirit who places every believer into a dynamic relationship with others in the body of Christ. Therefore, our job is to guard and preserve the unity that God has already given us.

Preserving Our Unity

That's why Ephesians 4:3 is so important. We quoted part of it earlier, but it's time to give the whole verse. Let me start with verse 1 to set the context: "Therefore I, the prisoner of the Lord, implore you to walk in a manner worthy of the calling with which you have been called." A big part of this worthy walk is "being diligent to preserve the unity of the Spirit in the bond of peace" (v. 3).

"Being diligent" means to make unity a top priority. The church's unity is already a reality. Our job is not to mess it up. Now if God is this serious about the church's unity, what would you call it when a believer decides this doesn't apply to him or her and blows off the fellowship of God's people? I would call it sin, because the church is not optional. It is essential.

Verses 11–16 of Ephesians 4 highlight the importance of the

church in God's plan and the importance of every believer contributing to its strength. Christ gave gifted people to the church (see v. 11) "for the equipping of the saints for the work of service, to the building up of the body of Christ; until we all attain to the unity of the faith" (vv. 12–13a). The emphasis throughout this section is on the growth of "the whole body" (v. 16) until every member of the church reaches spiritual maturity. That's a lifelong assignment because there is always room for growth and because this growth requires the participation of every member of the body for it to occur as it should.

Comparing the church to a human body really helps us to see how vital unity is to the church's health and growth. The old people used to say that if someone wasn't in church, something was missing. They understood in a more profound way than we do today that it takes "the proper working of each individual part" (Ephesians 4:16) to make the church go and grow. So if Sister or Brother Jones was absent, the rest of the body felt the loss of the missing part.

You sometimes hear people argue that their failure to be part of a church isn't hurting anyone because there are plenty of other people there. But if Paul is right in Ephesians 4 that each part of the body is essential, then those people must be wrong. If they are true believers and therefore have been baptized into the body of Christ by the Holy Spirit, they *are* damaging the body's unity and functioning by their absence.

The dreaded disease of cancer is the best illustration of what can happen when even a few cells in the body refuse to go along with the program. Cancer begins with rebel cells that want to go their own way. And they are not content to rebel themselves. They quickly reproduce after their own kind because disunity never likes to do its work alone. That's why people who sow disunity are always gossips. They want to create as big a mess as they can. When enough cancer cells are produced, now the victim has a lump to deal with.

And what's even worse than cancer cells reproducing in one part of the body is their tendency to invade other parts. Cancer only has one agenda, which is to shut the victim down, to cause the body to cease its functioning. That's why cancer treatments often have to be so radical. If you don't kill the cancer, it will kill you. Doctors know that if cancer is allowed to disrupt the body's unity, the whole body is threatened with destruction.

So it is with the faith of Jesus Christ. Every part of Christ's body has to cooperate with the program if the church is going to be everything that God wants us to be.

Here in Texas we have to deal with fire ants, which can build mounds of unbelievable size in fields that are not treated regularly. And even when we treat the small ant hills that pop up in our lawns, we really don't rid ourselves of the ants. They simply move underground and come out elsewhere. Trying to ignore them doesn't work, because those mounds are right there on the lawn. And stamping on them doesn't do any good because they just scatter and come back together as soon as you're gone.

Apparently these ants had a meeting at some point and decided that, while they are so tiny and insignificant by themselves that they can't bother anybody, they can present a serious presence and really stir things up when they unify. We as Christians need to have the same kind of meeting, because if God's people ever got together we would exert an influence for Christ on this world that could not be ignored or stamped out. But this requires that we give up being "Mr. Big Stuff" and realize that we are absolutely nothing apart from God's grace.

"Cruise Ship" Christians

If I can change the analogy, one of the problems we have in the church today that threatens our unity and effectiveness is what I call the "cruise ship" approach to Christianity.

Now I have to tell you, I love cruises. As I write this, several of the major cruise lines are having terrible problems with passengers getting sick on their voyages. But setting that aside for the moment, going on a cruise is my all-time favorite vacation.

Do you know why it's so wonderful to go on a cruise? Because somebody else does everything for you. You don't even have to handle your luggage. The crew provides recreation and serves you about eight meals a day with fabulous food. And if you don't want to get out of bed, that's fine. They'll bring the food to your room. They'll even wash and iron your clothes. Every detail on a cruise ship is designed to pamper you, and all you have to do is decide how much you want to enjoy.

The problem is that this cruise ship mentality has invaded the church, so people expect to be fed and entertained. They say, "I think I'll cruise on over to church this morning and see what they have for me. I'll check out the music menu and see if there's anything I like. I'll find out what they're serving on the Bible study menu and sample the sermon buffet."

This is a problem because the church is a battleship, not a cruise ship. When a battleship engages the enemy, what is the call that goes out? "All hands to their duty stations." Every person on a battleship earns his keep by doing a job that's vital to the ship's victory in battle.

Now the interesting thing is that the same folk who treat the church like a cruise ship will also come to the church's leaders and say, "I need help from the deacons' fund." Our church has a deacons' fund that we use to help people in need. When people ask for money from this fund, we ask them what ministry they are serving in at church. If they stutter and hesitate, we know we have a problem. You see, we don't just take people's word for it when they say they are doing this or that service. We check with the leaders in charge of that particular ministry. If there is no attempt on their part to contribute to the life and unity of the body, we are going to deal with that before giving them money. We are committed to the idea that people cannot say to the church, "Do this and this for me," while not being willing to do anything for the body themselves.

Paul said something profoundly important about Christ's body, the church, in 1 Corinthians 12: "If one member suffers, all the members suffer with it; if one member is honored, all the members rejoice with it" (v. 26). I can't emphasize often enough that we as Christians are joined together in a vital, living, organic unity that is indispensable to the church's proper functioning.

Without thinking about it, you illustrated this unity that night you stubbed your toe on the coffee table walking through the living room in the dark. When you heard that crunch and felt that blinding shot of pain race through your body, all systems came alive. Your nerves sent a message to your brain, "Searing pain in right big toe." Your brain then sent a message to your left arm: "Grab right toe and hold it up," and another message to your left leg: "Get ready, all the weight is coming your way, and start dancing around." Finally, a message went to your mouth, "Open wide and let everybody else in the house know that you just stubbed your toe." Your whole body reacted to one member that was suffering because everything is connected.

The same kind of thing happens when you are being honored. Your brain tells your face to smile and your mouth to say, "Thank you." The message goes to your arms to reach out and accept the award and to grasp the hand of the person presenting the award in a warm handshake. Your brain tells your heart to beat just a little faster so you will know something exciting is happening, and it may tell your knees to feel a little weak so you will sense that this is a special moment to savor. You also get a message to express love toward those people who helped you achieve this honor.

Whether you are hurting or rejoicing, your entire body reacts because the parts are connected. This is how the church is designed to work too.

Loving One Another

One final passage that's important for this study is Colossians 3:14, where Paul wrote: "Beyond all these things put on love, which is the perfect bond of unity." Notice the language of priority again. Love is not optional because the church's unity is not optional.

This verse answers the question of how we can practice true Christian unity with people we may not particularly like. Our likes and dislikes are personal preferences, which is why the Bible never commands us to like anybody. We are commanded to love one another, however, because biblical love has nothing to do with preferences or feelings. It is a decision of our will to act in the best interest of another person, even at our expense. The Bible is so radical on this that the apostle John told the church, "The one who does not love his brother whom he has seen, cannot love God whom he has not seen" (1 John 4:20). If you say, "Tony, down deep in my heart I just don't feel the importance of this unity thing," then it's time to test your "love quotient" for your fellow believers. Unity is the result of genuine love. Paul said unity is perfected in love.

A lot of us used to fuss and fight with our siblings when we were growing up. But it was a different story when someone else started messing with the family. My brother might not have liked me at a particular moment when we were fussing, but don't let someone else get on me. We had a blood bond working for us. The church has a blood bond working among its members too—the blood of Jesus Christ, which has bonded all of us into the same family. Let's make sure we are building up and not tearing down the unity of the church.

13

THE
SERVICE
OF THE
CHURCH

The story is told of a woman who was given a free trip to Europe. On the flight overseas, one of the airline's flight attendants became ill and couldn't serve the passengers. The flight was packed full and the crew was desperately trying to serve everyone. This woman went to the head of the flight crew and volunteered to help serve the meal, telling her, "I'm so happy and grateful to have this free trip to Europe that I don't mind at all serving on the way over."

The message is clear to those of us who know Jesus Christ. Our salvation and our trip to heaven are free, paid for in full by the blood of Christ. In gratitude for what God has given us, we ought not mind at all serving Him on the way over. Among all the names and titles we carry as believers, we are "bond-servants of Christ Jesus" (Philippians 1:1). That's what Paul called himself and his ministry companions, and I don't mind being identified with that group.

In this chapter I want to consider four aspects of the church's calling to serve God, other believers, and the people around us. Serving others is not just a nice thing to do at the holidays or during times of special outreach. It's a way of life for those of us who claim the name of Christ. Let's remind ourselves of what Jesus said concerning His disciples and even Himself: "Whoever wishes to become great among you shall be your servant; and whoever wishes to be first among you shall be slave of all. For even the Son of Man did not come to be served, but to serve, and to give His life a ransom for many" (Mark 10:43–45). The church that wants to enjoy God's blessing must be a place where the members understand their role as servants and are ready to roll up their sleeves to serve in Christ's name and His love.

OUR MANDATE TO SERVE

I want you to understand first of all that service for Christians is a mandate from God, which means it is mandatory. We love to talk about how we are free in Christ from all the restraints and restrictions of the Mosaic Law, and that is absolutely true. But Paul cautioned the believers in Galatia not to take their freedom too far: "You were called to freedom, brethren; only do not turn your freedom into an opportunity for the flesh, but through love serve one another" (Galatians 5:13).

Elsewhere, Paul told Christian slaves, "With good will render service, as to the Lord, and not to men" (Ephesians 6:7). The Greek word for *slaves* is the same as "bond-servants" in Philippians 1:1, which includes every believer regardless of our status on earth. All of us are mandated, or commanded, to serve.

Serving the Right Person

You may be saying, "Being a servant or a slave doesn't sound like a really exciting calling." Oh, but it is, when you are serving the right person with the right tools. The legendary pop singer Bob Dylan wrote a song some years ago called "Gotta Serve Somebody." We're going to talk about our motivation for service later in the chapter, so let me just say that when you are doing your service "as to the Lord, and not to men," that changes everything. Christ is the right Person, and the right tools are the spiritual gifts given to every member of Christ's body.

We've become familiar with Ephesians 4:7–16, a passage that has much to teach us about the divine nature and proper functioning of the church. The Bible says, "To each one of us grace was given according to the measure of Christ's gift" (v. 7). Every believer is gifted for service, which is why Paul said that Christ gave His gifts "for the equipping of the saints for the work of service, to the building up of the body of Christ" (v. 12). There is no such thing in the Bible as a saint who doesn't serve.

Sandwiched between these verses is Paul's recounting of Christ's triumphant return to heaven after defeating sin and the devil at the cross and rising from the dead. Jesus went into Satan's domain and led the righteous saints from the Old Testament era out of the paradise side of Hades into heaven. These were the people who put their faith in the coming Messiah and died without seeing the fulfillment of God's promise in the life, death, and resurrection of Christ. Christ led them into glory like a triumphant Roman general returning from battle with his captives in his train.

This is exactly the imagery that Paul drew on here. Now notice that in addition to leading His captives, Jesus also dispensed gifts to His people. A conquering general in the ancient world also came back from battle loaded down with spoils from the enemy, which he then bestowed on his friends and put to use to benefit his country.

On the cross, the Lord Jesus Christ defeated the devil. His resurrection proved this, becoming God's "receipt" to show that He accepted in full the payment Christ made for sin. Besides defeating the devil, Christ also spoiled Satan's kingdom and bestowed gifts to His friends, the people who confess Him as their Savior and Lord. In so doing, Christ placed within every believer a gifting, a unique ability blended with each person's personality, background, experiences, and training. He intends for these gifts to become the vehicle through which He expresses Himself for the building up of the church.

Serving with the Right Tools

What is a spiritual gift? It is a divine endowment, or a divinely bestowed ability, that God gives to each of His people to serve the rest of His body. The Bible clearly teaches that every saint has been gifted for service, without exception. Some may have more gifts than others, but all of the gifts are to be used to strengthen the church "until we all attain . . . to a mature man, to the measure of the stature which belongs to the fullness of Christ" (Ephesians 4:13).

As we saw in the previous chapter, the body of Christ grows to the extent that each part is working properly. This means that every saint is critical. No believer is an addendum or an afterthought in the body of Christ. Your contribution and mine, through our divine enablement or gifting, are important if the whole body is to grow and reach maturity.

Today we are used to specialists in every field who perform very specific tasks and are looked upon as being at the top of their field. But Jesus Christ has a specialized role for every believer to fulfill in the church. No one else has your unique blend of personality, experience, and gifts, and God has a place designed for you.

That doesn't mean that if you don't use your gifts, or I don't use mine, the job won't ultimately get done. God will see to it that His will is accomplished. But that's not where we are told to put our focus. Our attitude should not be, "Oh well, if I don't do it, no sweat. Someone else will." If we don't serve, we will lose reward and blessing, and hinder the work of the church that would have benefited from our service.

Most of us don't think about our bodies until some part stops functioning the way it should. Then we find we aren't feeling well and can't do what we ordinarily do. In the same way, a local church will only be as strong as the service of its members through their spiritual gifting. You need to understand that if you are not serving in the church, you are not only draining some of the vitality from the body of Christ, but you are weakening yourself because you are also a member of the same body. A body part that refuses to work, or a group of cells that decides to rebel against the program, becomes an enemy of the body instead of an ally.

THE MEASURE OF OUR SERVICE

You may have noticed in Ephesians 4 that Paul twice used the word *measure* in relation to the giving of spiritual gifts for the building up of Christ's body. One reference is to the "measure of Christ's gift" and the second is "the measure of the stature which belongs to the fullness of Christ" (vv. 7, 13).

Christ Is Our Standard

The point is hard to miss. The measure, or the standard, of our service is Christ Himself. This means, for instance, that we don't have to compare ourselves to other Christians and wonder why they were given certain gifts that we didn't get. It also means that Christ is the One we are working to please, not someone else. More on that later.

Of course, true service done in Christ's name and power will be pleasing to others, but their reaction is not the standard. Christ alone is the measure—or more specifically, the "fullness of Christ," which basically means that our service should make us and those we serve as much like Christ as it is possible to be in this life.

Measuring Ourselves for Service

Christ is our measure in terms of the goal or standard we are to work toward. But there is another sense in which we are told to measure our service for Christ, and for that we need to look at Romans 12. This is the great passage that begins with our responsibility to worship God by presenting ourselves to Him as a "living and holy sacrifice" who is ready to "prove what the will of God is" (vv. 1–2).

Most people stop reading with verse 2 because these two verses are so familiar. But verse 3 begins with "for," which is a connecting word. Paul has more to say to the Romans, and to us, on this subject. And what he is going to say in verses 3–8 is that our commitment to worship and seek God's will isn't complete until we are ready to serve. In other words, if your worship does not lead to service, then you haven't finished worshiping yet.

In verse 3 we are told, "For through the grace given to me I say to everyone among you not to think more highly of himself than he ought to think; but to think so as to have sound judgment, as God has allotted to each a measure of faith." This is not saving faith, but a capacity to serve. Every Christian has been given grace that is designed to lead to God-honoring service in the church. But before we can serve effectively, there is a standard of thinking we must adopt by which to measure our service.

Paul called this thinking with "sound judgment" so that we do not get inflated egos and begin to think more highly of ourselves than we should. If we're not careful, we can begin to think that the church is fortunate to have us and our gifts. Or, even worse, we can get the idea that service is beneath us, that it's for other people who aren't as important as we are.

The other side of the coin is thinking more lowly of ourselves than we should, but that's not a problem that most believers wrestle with. However, there is such a thing as false humility that causes people to insist that they really can't do anything when God has gifted them in some measure. If God has given you a gift to use in His service, use it and don't apologize for it.

Finding Our Place to Serve

Thinking with sound judgment also means that we are realistic about our gifts and our ability to serve. The problem is that some Christians want to serve where they were never meant to serve. That is, if you tremble at the thought of people being in your house and you have no idea what to do with them, you may not have the gift of hospitality. If you are terrified at the prospect of getting up in front of a group of people and trying to teach, it's a good possibility you don't have the spiritual gift of teaching.

Now don't misunderstand. Not having a particular gift doesn't excuse you from serving. Every Christian should be hospitable, for example, whether that's an individual's gift or not. All Christians are commanded to be Christ's witnesses, although there is a gift of evangelism that some believers clearly have.

What I'm talking about is finding the area of service where God has called and equipped you. When you are functioning in your area of giftedness there will be a joy and freedom and blessing to your service that may not be there if you are trying to fit a square peg into a round hole. The measure of our service is the capacity God has given us to find our place in His body where we can bless Him and others by the service we render.

It's important that all of us serve up to our capacity, because this thing of being a Christian is not just about us. Paul continued in Romans 12: "For just as we have many members in one body and all the members do not have the same function, so we, who are many, are one body in Christ, and individually members one of another. Since we have gifts that differ according to the grace given to us, each of us is to exercise them accordingly" (vv. 4–6a).

Here we are again, coming back to the interconnectedness of Christ's body the church. How important is it that each member does his or her part? It's vitally important, because no two of us have exactly the same function. A non-serving saint is like an ear on the human body that decides it doesn't want to hear anything today, or a hand that decides it has done too much and is going to take the day off. Let one of your ears or hands quit working, and your whole body will suffer.

I want to make a statement that you may consider controversial. Any Christian who is not a functioning, serving member of a local church is living outside of the will of God. Now this certainly doesn't mean that all of our service has to take place within the four walls of the church building. For instance, many churches have elderly, homebound believers who pray faithfully. And a young mother is serving the Lord as she takes care of her children. My point is that the Bible says that each member is to serve according to the measure of faith God has given. Failing to serve when God has given the capacity is to disobey His will. The list of spiritual gifts in Romans 12:6b–8 makes it clear that whatever your gift may be, the thing to do is get after it with everything you have. If you are going to teach, determine to be the best teacher your class has ever had. If you are going to give, give generously.

Some people will only exercise their gifts if they get paid for it. I believe there are some Christians using their God-given spiritual gifts and abilities on their jobs who aren't willing to donate these gifts to God's kingdom. So the world gets their best while the body of Christ derives no benefit from them.

I like what Paul said in Romans 12 about being willing to serve because of the grace given to us. God doesn't want you to serve just because it is commanded. He wants you to serve because of His grace poured out in your life. The more you understand grace, the easier it is to serve. Grace is all that God has done for you without charging you anything. That's a lot of grace, enough to keep you for all eternity. When you and I put our service up against the measurement of God's grace, there is nothing we can do but serve Him gladly with our whole hearts.

THE MANIFESTATION OF OUR SERVICE

Another key passage that addresses our service in the context of God's gifts is 1 Corinthians 12. I want to pick up two verses that we need to fix in our minds as we talk about the church's service, the first of which is verse 7. After saying that there are varieties of gifts, ministries, and effects (vv. 4–6), Paul added the clincher: "But to each one is given the manifestation of the Spirit for the common good" (v. 7).

The Holy Spirit's Imprint

I am often asked how to tell the difference between people who are simply operating in their own natural ability and strength and those whose efforts are truly being used by God for His glory. The answer is found in 1 Corinthians 12:7. First of all, if our service is from God, no matter what it is, then the Holy Spirit's fingerprints will be all over it. And second, if it is from God, then it will be done for the "common good" of the body of Christ and not just for personal gain or recognition.

Let me explain what I mean. The Bible doesn't say anything about a specific spiritual gift of singing. Most good singers are born with a God-given ability that other folk simply don't have. And a person doesn't have to be a Christian to have a God-given voice. But all of us know the difference between listening to someone sing for entertainment and hearing someone whose talent is dedicated to God's service and whose singing is anointed by the Holy Spirit. The first singer simply used a talent. But the Holy Spirit manifested Himself through the second singer's music.

It is the manifestation of the Holy Spirit that makes any gift or ability unique. When you and I are trying to operate outside of our giftedness, or when we are exercising our gifts in our fleshly strength apart from the Sprit's enabling, nothing happens because the Spirit is not manifesting Himself. And when there is no manifestation of the Spirit, we will not see God at work in supernatural power in and through us.

This is why so much of the service we see being carried out in so many churches produces so little lasting impact. If we are not operating in conscious dependence upon the Holy Spirit and allowing Him to work through us, then we are exercising our abilities and talents to no real purpose. Sinners can exercise great natural abilities and carry out acts of service. Sinners can sing, teach, feed the hungry, and do all of the other things that Christians can do.

But sinners cannot manifest the Holy Spirit, and He is the only One who can take what we do and produce results that human ability alone can never account for. In other words, an unbeliever can stir people by a great song or a great speech. But when God uses a person who doesn't have great skills to lead scores to Christ, it is obvious that something greater than the human vessel is at work. We've all heard stories of missionaries whom the world considered weak and insignificant, but whom God used to shake nations and continents for Him.

I hope you have had the thrilling experience of seeing God take what you do for Him and use it far beyond what you ever imagined He could. That's when you know it isn't you or your abilities, because you know that you weren't able in your own strength to pull off what just happened. If God isn't doing anything through you that can only be explained by the Spirit's manifestation in your life, get on your knees and ask Him to help you get started.

And, by the way, when the Holy Spirit is manifesting Himself through your service, you will not be the only one who sees it. The people you are serving will know that you have been used of God for their benefit. That's why the corporate ministry of the church is indispensable, for at least three reasons.

First, the church provides the context in which we serve each other and the world around us. The Holy Spirit is going to have a hard time manifesting Himself in the life of a Christian who is living in spiritual isolation.

Second, the church is also indispensable because when a local body of believers in whom the Spirit is working comes together, His power is multiplied and expanded.

Third, we need the church because it is a group of people in whom the Holy Spirit is able to manifest Himself in many different ways. This gets back to the church's connectedness. We need the whole body so that the whole ministry of Christ is accomplished. If everyone in the church was a preacher, there's a lot that would never get done. In 1 Corinthians 12:14–21, Paul addressed this issue by saying that if the body were all eyes, ears, or feet, vital functions would be left undone. A local church with non-serving saints is suffering like a human body that is missing an eye, an ear, or a foot.

The Holy Spirit's Choice

There is another way that the Spirit manifests Himself in the church's service. According to 1 Corinthians 12:11, "One and the same Spirit works all these things, distributing to each one individually just as He wills." The "things" mentioned here are the spiritual gifts of verses 8–10, which of course is just a partial list. The Spirit sovereignly gives each believer the exact gift or combination of gifts He wants that person to have.

So don't get mad or jealous if the Christian next to you at church has a spiritual gift you wish you had, and are convinced you could do a better job with anyway! Take it up with the Holy Spirit. He decides who receives what gift, because He knows each one of us intimately, far better than we know ourselves, and He can see how we will best serve the kingdom with our personality and background. The Spirit doesn't need our counsel or input on His decision—and besides, remember that the goal of the church's spiritual gifting is to promote "the common good" (1 Corinthians 12:7), not our personal preferences.

I mentioned earlier that our son Jonathan is currently at Baylor University in Waco, Texas, on a football scholarship. Jonathan had been an all-district tight end in high school, but the coach at Baylor told him, "Our team needs you at fullback."

Now the facts that Jonathan had never played fullback, didn't think of himself as a fullback, and didn't really want to be a fullback were irrelevant, because the coach made the decision as he willed based on his experience and Jonathan's size and skills. Jonathan wasn't sure how he would do at a new position, but the coach saw something in Jonathan that he himself didn't see. And after a year learning the position, Jonathan is slated to be Baylor's starting fullback.

The Holy Ghost knows your propensities, strengths, and weaknesses, so He knows just where to place you in the lineup, so to speak. You will never see God move in your life as you will when you allow Him to use the gifts He has given you to serve others. As a pastor, it boggles my mind to think of what would happen if an entire body of believers in a local church decided to get on the Holy Spirit's team and play where He tells them to play. The world couldn't stand against us!

I know what someone is thinking at this point. *When the Holy Spirit shows me what my gift is, then I'll start serving.* No, you start serving and the Spirit will reveal your gift to you. He only hits a moving target. Make yourself available to the church in the areas of your interests and abilities, and the Spirit will show you whether you are operating in the area of your giftedness.

This reminds me of Moses at the burning bush. When God told him to go to Egypt and deliver the Israelites from slavery, Moses made a series of objections (see Exodus 3:11–4:17). Let me summarize the conversation in my own words. It began when God said, "Moses, go tell Pharaoh to let My people go."

"But Lord, who am I to deliver such a message?"

"I will be with you."

"But what if the Israelites ask me Your name? I won't know what to tell them."

"Tell them I Am Who I Am has sent you."

"OK, but what if they don't believe me?"

"Here are some signs to convince them. Throw down your staff and it will become a serpent, and when you pick it up it will become a stick again. Put your hand in your robe and pull it out, and it will have leprosy. Do it again, and your hand will be clean. And if they still don't believe you, take some water from the Nile river, pour it on the ground, and it will become blood."

"But Lord, You can't be serious. I've never been a good public speaker. My mouth doesn't work right."

"I will be with your mouth and teach you what to say."

"Lord, I can't do this. Send somebody else!"

By now Moses was really ticking God off (see Exodus 4:14). "I'll send Aaron with you, and I will work with both of your mouths. Now go!"

Moses didn't see God's delivering power until he went to Pharaoh and opened his mouth. But when he obeyed and served God, Moses discovered he had "ten plague" power. Don't try to tell God when and under what conditions you will serve. Find something to do at church that you have an interest in, that God has laid on your heart, or that you feel you have the ability to do, and get going. God will show you where He has uniquely blessed you.

If I had been counseled for a career on the basis of my speech, no one would have told me to consider being a pastor. I had a massive speech impediment when I was in elementary and junior high school. I stammered terribly, which they called back then being "tongue-tied." I couldn't carry on a conversation. But even though I could barely get a consonant out of my mouth without stumbling, God had placed a gifting within me.

As I grew up, I had a burning desire to tell people about Christ. I discovered that when I was talking about Jesus or the Bible the words would flow, even though I still had trouble in normal conversation. Something happened when the manifestation of the Spirit took over that was beyond my human ability. When we serve with the gifts the Holy Spirit has given us in dependence upon Him, He manifests His power in and through us.

THE MOTIVATION FOR OUR SERVICE

Along with all of the other blessings that accompany our service to and with the body of Christ, there is a wonderful motivation that can keep us going when all the other props are knocked out from under us.

Peter gave us this motivation when he wrote,

As each one has received a special gift, employ it in serving one another as good stewards of the manifold grace of God. Whoever speaks, is to do so as one who is speaking the utterances of God; whoever serves is to do so as one who is serving by the strength which God supplies; *so that in all things God may be glorified through Jesus Christ, to whom belongs the glory and dominion forever and ever.* Amen. (1 Peter 4:10–11, italics added)

Serving for God's Glory

We need to understand that our service for the Lord, and the gifts with which to do it, are a stewardship from God, the One for whose ultimate glory we serve. Of course, we are called to serve one another, as we talked about earlier. But we have to be straight about our true motivation, because if you and I are serving only for people, we are going to crash at some point.

Why? Because not everyone will appreciate us, even in the church. Not everyone is going to say thank you or treat us right, even when our motivation was to do right. Unless we serve with our eyes on the Lord, some people somewhere along the line are going to make us want to quit. That's just the truth of human nature, even redeemed human nature. Our motive to serve has to be for God and His glory. And the great thing is that He never misreads our motive or overlooks the least act of service done for Him.

Receiving God's Reward

There is also a great motivational principle for us in Colossians 3:22–24. Paul exhorted slaves to serve their masters well, not simply to please them "but with sincerity of heart, fearing the Lord. Whatever you do, do your work heartily, as for the Lord rather than for men, knowing that from the Lord you will receive the reward of the inheritance. It is the Lord Christ whom you serve."

This speaks directly to our work, but it also has application to our service in the church. If you're content to have people reward you with a pat on the back or nice words, then you will serve with that temporary reward in view. There's nothing wrong with being recognized and appreciated for faithful service rendered, but we have a much greater prize to keep our eyes on—the reward that Jesus will give us when we stand before Him.

Another great thing about serving with the goal to please God is that He doesn't use the world's measure to judge our service. The world may reward those who are out front or who make the biggest splash, but God considers those in the background to be equally valuable and important. That's why Jesus said the last will be first someday.

Let me also add a word about something that is very important to me. The fact that we are serving our great God for His eternal glory means that we ought to serve with excellence. Christians should be the best workers on the job. The boss ought to be asking his Christian employees, "Are there any more at home like you? If there are, send them in here." Nobody wants to be treated by a slipshod physician. Your employer doesn't appreciate sloppy service, and God doesn't appreciate sloppy saints. Please don't tell folk you are working for the Lord and then do the job halfway.

You may say, "I can't really give my attention to excellence in everything I do because I'm involved in so many things." If that's the case, you need to hear Jesus' words to His dear friend, Martha of Bethany: "Martha, Martha, you are worried and bothered about so many things; but only one thing is necessary" (Luke 10:41–42). Martha was trying to fix a huge meal when one dish would have been enough, and that was a problem because Martha's busyness was keeping her from spending time with the Lord.

I don't know if you are plugged in to a local church, but I can tell you that saints who aren't serving are missing out on seeing the Spirit of God move in their lives and strengthening the life of the church. A lot of people are perpetual church visitors because that way they can avoid taking any responsibility to serve. They keep visiting so they can enjoy the church's ministry without having to pour out their lives for the good of other believers and the glory of God.

Yes, people ought to visit a church before they join and make a commitment to serve. But it doesn't take two years to decide if a church is the right one. If we want the smile and the blessing of God on our lives, then He would tell us to serve the body of Christ with our whole hearts for the church's good and His glory. Heavenly reward is wonderful to think about, but it is the fruit of faithful service. Bringing God glory is an exciting prospect, but it doesn't happen in a vacuum. I hope you can say that the church you attend is stronger because you are serving.

14

THE ACCOUNTABILITY OF THE CHURCH

I'm sure I speak for many parents when I say that the births of our children were among the greatest moments of my life. There is nothing like hearing the doctor say, "It's a boy," or, "You've got a little girl." Each of my four children is a unique blessing, and each birth was an exciting event. I loved holding those little babies that were put into my hands.

But I soon discovered there was a downside to being a father, which is known as dirty diapers. I was big on holding my children. I was not big on changing and cleaning them up. That was an area it took my wife a long time to disciple me in.

New births are exciting, but the messes that come with new life are not. Dealing with them is a necessary part of life, however, whether we are talking about a human family or the family of God. There's nothing like seeing people come to Christ. In our church people get excited and applaud when a new spiritual birth has taken place. But with life also comes the inevitable need to deal with the "dirty diapers" of problems that all saints have as imperfect beings.

THE NECESSITY OF ACCOUNTABILITY

Because life brings problems, one of the church's important ministries is to call its members to be accountable for the way they live. This may involve teaching and encouraging the saints in their walk with the Lord, and at times it may involve applying biblical discipline to a sinning saint for the purpose of correction and restoration.

But whatever form accountability takes, the church cannot escape its responsibility to see that its members are living lives worthy of Christ (see Ephesians 4:1). When we do this, we are imitating our Lord: "For whom the Lord loves He disciplines, and He scourges every son whom He receives" (Hebrews 12:6).

The work of discipline and restoration is part of the church's discipleship training, but it is also one of the most difficult and neglected areas of church ministry. We are terrified by the very thought of having to practice discipline. We're afraid of what people might think or do, which is why some parents are afraid to discipline their children. But discipline is a non-negotiable in Scripture.

I am going to make a strong statement here that I believe can be substantiated biblically. A church that does not practice discipline of its members is not yet functioning properly as a church, just as a family that does not discipline is not a fully functioning family. The writer of Hebrews went on to say, "It is for discipline that you endure; God deals with you as with sons; for what son is there whom his father does not discipline? But if you are without discipline, of which all have become partakers, then you are illegitimate children and not sons" (12:7–8). A church that lets its people go around undisciplined has no real claim to be part of God's family. You cannot raise a healthy family without accountability and discipline.

Directive Discipline

Accountability in the church can take two basic forms, which we could call directive and corrective. Directive discipline has to do with the church pointing out the way that people should go, directing them in the way of godliness. The church does this by exercising its ministry of teaching, encouraging, and exhorting the saints to deal with sin and live holy and fruitful lives.

This may involve correction in the form of pointing out what is wrong so people can fix it and get back on the right path. But I'm reserving the term "corrective discipline" for the action that needs to be taken when a believer refuses to go in the right direction and persists in sin. Directive discipline has a much more positive implication. It's what happens when believers respond to the church's ministry and seek to get their lives lined up with Christ.

This is where the ministries of the church come in. We have already talked about this at length, so let me just say that a church ought to have a ministry of some kind for each need represented in its congregation, whether it's single parents, people needing job skills and/or placement, or marriage and family issues.

A common response to this is, "We don't have enough people in our church to do all of those things." That may be true in some cases, but what this often means is that the church doesn't have enough members who are committed to serving the body. That's a different problem than saying you're short-handed. The root of discipline is discipleship, and the church's main job is to make disciples. Directive discipline requires the involvement of the entire body of Christ.

Corrective Discipline

When a believer rejects the church's directive discipline and decides to continue in a sinful direction, the church is to apply corrective discipline. This application of discipline revolves around the refusal to deal with sin, what the Bible calls "presumptuous sin." The

Old Testament law made this stipulation: "The man who acts presumptuously by not listening to the priest who stands there to serve the Lord your God, nor to the judge, that man shall die; thus you shall purge the evil from Israel" (Deuteronomy 17:12).

The saint who will not listen to the church and its duly appointed leaders is a candidate for corrective discipline. If a person won't hold himself accountable for his sin, it's up to the church to hold him accountable. It's the spirit of rebellion behind the sin that needs to be dealt with as much as, or perhaps more than, the fact of the sin.

The Necessity of Judging

Before we get to the process of church discipline, we need to deal with a common objection, which sounds spiritual on the surface. As soon as we mention church discipline, someone will quote Jesus' statement: "Do not judge so that you will not be judged" (Matthew 7:1). This sounds very spiritual at first, but the problem is that nobody reads on to verses 2–5. Jesus did *not* say we are not to judge under any circumstances. His warning was against hypocritical judgment, someone with a "log" in his eye passing judgment on someone with a "speck" in his eye (v. 3).

In other words, Jesus' concern was making sure that we are qualified to judge. He said, "First take the log out of your own eye, and then you will see clearly to take the speck out of your brother's eye" (v. 5). Instead of prohibiting judgment, Jesus told us to make sure we are judging righteously. Judging situations and practicing discipline is necessary if we are to make a distinction between what is right and wrong.

Paul told Timothy that the Word of God is profitable "for reproof [and] for correction," and then commanded Timothy to "reprove" the people under his charge (2 Timothy 3:16; 4:2). Making necessary judgments is part of what the church does, because a church is responsible to bring its members to full maturity in Christ.

THE DETAILS OF DISCIPLINE

The basic rules for carrying out discipline in the church were established before the church ever came into existence. The Savior and Lord of the church set this standard in Matthew 18:15–20, the central passage for church discipline. Other texts speak to the subject, but Jesus' teaching here is foundational because the responsibility given to the church is clearly spelled out.

The Participants in Discipline

First of all, look at the participants in discipline. Jesus said, "If your brother sins, go and show him his fault in private" (Matthew 18:15). Sin in the church is a family matter. The discipline that Jesus outlined is not for outsiders. I don't discipline the neighbors' children or expect them to live by my rules. But it was a different story for my kids when they lived at home.

The offender is not the only participant, of course. Any believer who sees a brother or sister fall into sin is responsible to go to that person and seek his or her restoration. Church discipline is not something to leave for the pastor or elders. If the offender refuses private discipline, then the process becomes more formal and involved because it requires "one or two more" people who can act as witnesses against the sin (v. 16).

These may be church leaders or members of the congregation. But if nothing else works to bring the sinner back, and if the church's leaders have not been involved to this point, they get involved now because the problem is brought "to the church" (v. 17). And if all avenues of discipline fail to bring about repentance and restoration, the leaders are the ones who announce to the church that this brother or sister is under discipline and is banned from the church's fellowship (see 1 Corinthians 5:9–11). So the level of participation goes in ever widening circles until the full church is involved if that becomes necessary.

When people join our church in Dallas, we tell them about our discipline process in the pre-membership class. We also require that they read and sign the church constitution, which includes our discipline procedures, before they are accepted into membership. In this way new members agree to come under the authority and, if necessary, the discipline of the church.

Before we go on, let me say a word about the love and compassion needed to execute discipline. If you see a brother or sister living in sin and you don't do anything about it, you are not acting toward the person in love. Why? Because chances are that if you don't reach out to the person, no one else will either. And if the brothers and sisters in a family don't look out for each other, then Daddy has to step in. And when Daddy disciplines, the other shoe drops.

So if we let a fellow believer go on in sin, we are saying, "I'll let Daddy deal with you." I don't know about your family, but in my family those were dreaded words because my father was a stern disciplinarian. When my daddy dealt with a child, it was all but over. Paul told the Corinthians that some of them had become sick and even died for abusing the Lord's Supper (see 1 Corinthians 11:29–30). Then he made this statement: "But if we judged ourselves rightly, we would not be judged" (v. 31).

If the discipline of a sinning saint has to go all the way to the Father in heaven, it is likely to be more severe than if we pull the offender back with a private rebuke. The reason for church discipline is to fix the problem before God has to come down from above and deal with it Himself.

The Problem Requiring Discipline

Jesus also gave the conditions under which discipline is to be initiated. It is sin that needs to be judged. Now that may seem obvious on paper, but it real life it isn't always so clear. In other words, what is *not* being judged here is personal preferences or biases, or hearsay about a person's alleged behavior with no proof. The issue is always sin, which is anything that violates the law of God. Discipline is not applied because someone did something that someone else doesn't like. Discipline is applied because someone did something that God doesn't like, and refuses to repent and come back.

The Bible distinguishes between the sins that we all commit and a lifestyle of persistent spiritual rebellion. For example, in Galatians 6:1, Paul advised, "Brethren, even if anyone is caught in any trespass, you who are spiritual, restore such a one in a spirit of gentleness; each one looking to yourself, so that you too will not be tempted."

This is a picture of someone being snared in a trap. In other words, the person Paul talked about here didn't set out to sin, but through the weakness of the flesh fell into the devil's trap. The sin is still serious, and the sinner needs to be restored. But he needs someone to cut him loose from the snare and set him free. And the one who is cutting him loose is warned to do this gently because he can also fall into a trap and be snared. The believer who is ensnared doesn't need discipline as we are talking about it, but loving release.

But in the case of open rebellion and known sin, the church's job is to bring the sin to light and deal with it. This begins with private rebuke and expands from there if that is not successful. Notice that this reproof is to be done face-to-face with the offender. Jesus said go to your brother, not to someone who knows your brother or to everybody else in the church but your brother.

Proper church discipline leaves no room for gossip or involving people who are not related to the problem, at least not until the whole church has to be notified of the discipline. The circle is kept as small as necessary because the objective at every level of discipline is restoration, not further harm. The goal is to win the offender back before things get worse.

This is serious stuff. Paul instructed Timothy, "Do not receive an accusation against an elder except on the basis of two or three witnesses. Those who continue in sin, rebuke in the presence of all, so that the rest also will be fearful of sinning" (1 Timothy 5:19–20). Even if the offender is an elder, he is to be publicly exposed and rebuked if necessary to deal with the sin.

This reminds me of Paul's public rebuke of Peter in Antioch (see Galatians 2:11–21). We referred to this incident earlier, when Peter allowed himself to be influenced by visitors from Jerusalem. He started pulling away from the Gentile believers, with whom he had been enjoying a ham sandwich, and his harmful behavior even encouraged Barnabas to do likewise. Paul rebuked Peter for hypocrisy and the hurt it caused to their Gentile brothers and sisters and to the cause of Christ.

Paul said, "I opposed [Peter] to his face, because he stood condemned" (Galatians 2:11). Paul didn't hold a workshop on racial reconciliation or offer a seminar on how to relate to Gentiles, because he was dealing with sin, not just a social problem. A lot of times we don't confront people because we don't want to treat the problem as sin. The reason America's race-relations problem has not been solved in 250 years is that it has been treated as a social problem to be fixed instead of sin to be confronted and repented of.

The Reasons to Discipline

We've touched on some of the reasons the Bible commands us to carry out discipline in the church. The first and most obvious is to teach the sinner the error of his ways. In 1 Timothy 1:20, Paul referred to two men named Hymenaeus and Alexander, "whom I have handed over to Satan, so that they will be taught not to blaspheme." Discipline has a teaching element to it. We must teach people not to take God or His Word lightly.

Discipline also teaches the rest of the body the seriousness of sin and the holiness of God. When I heard my brother getting a spanking, it made me change my mind about some of my plans. We read earlier that an elder who continues in sin is to be rebuked in the presence of everyone, so that others will fear.

A third reason for discipline is to restore the sinner. This may involve having to expose the person to public shame if everything else fails. We see this in 2 Thessalonians 3, where Paul was dealing with unruly members of the church: "If anyone does not obey our instruction in this letter, take special note of that person and do not associate with him, so that he will be put to shame" (v. 14). There is shame in being publicly rebuked and disciplined. But don't miss the purpose of the shame: "Yet do not regard him as an enemy, but admonish him as a brother" (v. 15).

Here's a reason for discipline we don't think much about today. Discipline shows the unrighteous world the church of God at work, so that the unrighteous will also fear God and His holiness. The sin of Ananias and Sapphira, described in Acts 5:1–11, not only had a profound effect on the church, but on everyone else in Jerusalem.

God killed these two not just because they lied, but for what they lied about. They said they had committed all the money from the sale of their property to the welfare of the church, when in fact they held back a part. Their lie damaged the body of Christ, and God won't tolerate those who try to destroy Christ's body (see 1 Corinthians 3:17).

Look at what happened after Ananias and Sapphira died. "Great fear came over the whole church, and over all who heard of these things" (Acts 5:11). This became known all over Jerusalem. The result was that "none of the rest dared to associate with [the church]" (v. 13). The unbelievers around the church said, "I'm not going to that church. Those folk are serious. You'd better think twice about joining that bunch." The church stood out from the culture because it corrected sin instead of tolerating or endorsing it.

THE PROCESS OF DISCIPLINE

The process of discipline is outlined clearly in Matthew 18:15–17. The first step is private confrontation of the offender by a caring fellow believer. The ideal situation is for the offender to respond to this loving and courageous act of caring.

Bringing Along Witnesses

But if the sinning saint does not respond, then the next step is to go to him in semi-private; that is, taking one or two others with you. This principle of requiring two or three witnesses to confirm a matter was well established in the Law (see Deuteronomy 19:15). This step validates the offender's sin and his refusal to repent. This rebellious attitude that refuses to address the sin, as opposed to struggling to deal with it, is the ultimate basis for church discipline.

Bringing in several other people protects against the process being a personal vendetta or making too much of a minor issue. If an accuser was simply trying to ruin another believer's reputation, or was overreacting, he should not be able to find other witnesses to help him. Now, of course, it is possible for people to get together and make something up. That happened with the false witnesses at Jesus' trial (see Mark 14:56). But multiple witnesses are still the best safeguard against one person trying to trump up a charge against someone. Otherwise, it could just be one person's word against another's.

Telling the Church

However, if the sinning saint refuses to listen to the two or three people who confront him and try to win him back, then the issue becomes a matter of public record. Jesus said, "Tell it to the church" (Matthew 18:17). I don't think this necessarily means announcing to the entire congregation that a member of the church is under discipline for unrepentant sin. The issue of how much of the church should be informed is a tough question. I believe the answer is that those people in the church who have the most direct access to and possible influence with the offender should be told so they can bring their influence to bear in trying to end the sin and turn the sinner back to the Lord.

On a practical level, this could be a Sunday school class or some other group in which the person under discipline is active. I don't believe Jesus' statement means that if you have two thousand people in your church, all two thousand need to be informed directly of the discipline being undertaken. It does mean, however, that the leadership is informed of the problem.

Now if there is a dispute about whether something does or does not qualify as a matter for church discipline, or if extenuating circumstances need to be considered, this is where the church court that I talked about earlier comes into play. The biblical basis for this court is in 1 Corinthians 6, where Paul clearly tells the church to take care of its own disputes, because it is a spiritual defeat and a mark against the name of Christ to take these things to the unrighteous.

I've said before that I believe a church court should be the rule in our churches instead of the exception. If one member of a married couple wants to get divorced and the other disputes the grounds, they can bring the case to our church court. The question is not whether the civil court feels the couple has grounds for divorce. The question is what God's Word says. Our church's court includes a person who has knowledge of the law, a godly layperson, and one of the leaders. We seek people who operate by biblical wisdom. They need to know what the Bible says and have wisdom to apply it in all situations.

If a person under discipline repents under the church's ministry, that's wonderful. But, in cases of extreme rebellion and refusal, the entire church may have to be informed, because the final stage of the church's judgment is to treat the offender "as a Gentile and a tax collector" (Matthew 18:17). Gentiles were outcasts because they were pagans. Tax collectors were Jews who were considered traitors because they served the Roman government by taking money from their fellow Jews.

So a stubbornly unrepentant believer is to be considered an outcast from the church, someone with whom the body is not to fellowship. This would seem to require that the congregation be informed of the rebellious person's judgment and banishment from the local body of Christ.

However the discipline is carried out, it has a formal side because the steps are endorsed and carried out by the leadership. Discipline is also informal because it involves the members going to each other as the need arises for confrontation.

THE POWER OF DISCIPLINE

Some people object that church discipline is a waste of time today because the disciplined person can just go down the street and join another church without changing his behavior at all. That may be true, but the objection misses the point that God commanded the church to practice discipline and that the power of church discipline is not limited to what we can see.

The Offender's Punishment

When Paul pronounced judgment on the man in Corinth who was having an affair with his stepmother, the apostle said: "I have decided to deliver such a one to Satan for the destruction of his flesh, so that his spirit may be saved in the day of the Lord Jesus" (1 Corinthians 5:5). If the offender will not listen to the church, maybe he will listen to the devil.

Some people who have been disciplined by the church don't seem to suffer the destruction of their flesh. But this phrase may mean more than just physical death, although that can certainly happen in extreme cases. There is a point of no return in sinful rebellion. John said there is a "sin leading to death" for which even prayer is useless (1 John 5:16).

The Bible also uses the word *flesh* to refer to a person's sinful appetites. Paul could be referring to the destruction of those appetites in the sense that a sinning believer who is turned over to Satan will find that the sinful pleasures which he refused to give up will turn on him and ravage him. Remember, the devil may allure us with pleasures and seem to offer a good time, but his goal is to ruin our lives and cause us to be lost forever.

This means there is a lot more going on in church discipline than meets the eye. The disciplined person may, as I said, just go somewhere else. But he still goes under the excommunication of the church if the discipline was legitimate. And that has consequences because Jesus said, "Truly I say to you, whatever you bind on earth shall have been bound in heaven; and whatever you loose on earth shall have been loosed in heaven" (Matthew 18:18).

Jesus was referring to the church's decision to expel a sinning member. So it doesn't matter if the offender goes to another church, he still goes there under discipline, and God says, "I will take it from here." Proper church discipline that has followed the biblical pattern means that the church is agreeing on earth to the decision that God has already made in heaven. The unrepentant sinner is bound by heaven, and God alone knows what steps heaven will take to chasten that person.

The Church's Excommunication

A believer who has resisted and refused the church's every effort at his repentance and restoration is a candidate for the very serious step of excommunication. I believe there is only one place where this step of discipline should be carried out, and that is around the communion table at the Lord's Supper. Why? Because the Bible makes it clear that this is where we deal with sin (see 1 Corinthians 11:27–32). This is one of the fundamental purposes of communion.

When we excommunicate a person from our church, we do so on Sunday morning in front of the whole congregation and around communion so that the rest may fear. And we have seen God work in amazing ways. One brother who went into wild living, divorced his wife, and refused to repent was removed from the church. His life fell apart, and after three years he called the church and said, "I want to repent and come home."

We met with him to examine his life and look for fruits of repentance, since we can't read people's hearts. When he had demonstrated his repentance, he was brought back to church on a Sunday morning. He stood before the church and apologized to the people. He also said that if his wife would have him back, he would like to come home to her and make up for the years that had been wasted.

The man's wife had been praying for him those three years and had not given up hope. I called her forward on this Sunday morning, and we performed the wedding right there in the middle of the service, amid a lot of crying and cheering.

THE JOY OF RESTORATION

Of course, it doesn't always happen this way. But this is the church being the church. And the church should rejoice when a lost sheep comes home.

We need to understand that God's restoration is often unlike ours. Sometimes we look at a repentant saint and say, "Yes, it's great that brother so-and-so has come back to the Lord. But he can't really ever be a full-fledged member of the church after what he has done."

I don't understand this thinking because the Bible deals with some pretty messy people who sinned greatly and were fully restored by God. This is not to say that sin is not serious or that it doesn't carry consequences. But when God restores a person, the restorations are sometimes staggering.

One example of this in story form is the Prodigal Son (see Luke 15:11–32). The father didn't banish his repentant son to the servant's quarters, but gave him back all the signs of sonship and threw a party. And lest you think this is just a story, let me remind you of the restoration of Peter by Jesus (see John 21:15–17).

There is no sin committed by a leader in Scripture that was any worse than Peter's sin, because Peter committed apostasy—the denial of the faith. At Jesus' trials and crucifixion Peter denied that he even knew Jesus. The Lord could have stripped Peter of his apostolic credentials and sent him packing.

But one morning after His resurrection, Jesus met Peter and some of the other disciples by the seashore. Jesus was cooking them breakfast on a charcoal fire (see v. 9), the same kind of fire at which Peter had denied him about a week earlier. Jesus was re-creating the scene of Peter's sin.

That's important because it shows that even though Jesus was there to restore Peter, He still took Peter's sin seriously. Peter needed to face what he had done. In fact, Jesus had Peter face his sin by asking him three times, "Do you love Me?" Peter responded each time, but by the third time he was upset that Jesus kept asking him. We remember, though, that Peter had denied Christ three times, so it was necessary that he affirm his love for Christ three times.

Jesus not only forgave and restored Peter, but gave him the pastoral assignment of feeding and leading the church. The next time we see Peter in action was the Day of Pentecost, when he preached the church's first sermon and led three thousand people to Christ. Then he opened the door of the church to the Gentiles when he preached to Cornelius in Acts 10. Peter experienced the joy of restoration, and he was never the same. The church should rejoice when a sinner comes home. Maybe we should even throw a party.

15

THE ORIENTATION OF THE CHURCH

The story is told of two boys who were raised in very different homes. The first boy grew up in a home where he had to follow his father's strict list of rules—or else! He received few hugs, few "I love yous," and very few positive messages from his father. The boy's total identity and acceptance were tied to his ability to live up to his father's rigid expectations.

Every night at dinner the boy's performance was evaluated, and he lived on pins and needles, always fearful of not meeting his father's demands or being condemned for his failures. And worse yet, the father did little to help his son meet the demands. Dad simply gave out the orders while remaining distant from his son. The boy became critical and negative himself.

The second boy was raised in a completely different kind of home. His father regularly affirmed his love for his son, demonstrating it with hugs and words of affirmation that let the boy know his value was based not on what he did or failed to do, but who he was. This boy and his father looked forward to being with each other, and they missed each other when they were apart. And while the father did have clear expectations of his son, he assisted and encouraged him in fulfilling them. This son grew up with a very positive spirit and felt a deep desire to please his father.

Not surprisingly, the first son loathed being in his family and counted the days until he could leave, while the second son loved his home and found it an encouraging and winsome place to live.

The difference between these two homes, and the resulting experiences of the two sons, illustrates the difference between law-based and grace-based churches. When a local church bases its ministry on law and rule-keeping rather than grace, spiritual growth is stunted and the church becomes an unpleasant, negative place to be. But when a church ministers the grace of God in all of its facets, it becomes an exciting, life-giving environment in which spiritual growth is nurtured. I'm afraid that, by and large, the church today sorely lacks a proper orientation toward grace.

That's tragic, because grace is the truth that makes Christianity different from every other religion in the world. Every religion on earth is predicated upon what its followers must do to make themselves acceptable to God. We call that a works orientation, and it doesn't matter whether you are talking about a particular branch of so-called Christendom, a pseudo-Christian cult, or a pagan religion. They are built on works. The deity only responds when the worshiper has made the proper sacrifice or offering or performed the proper act.

But the true faith of Christ is built on the fact that in Christ, God has taken the initiative to save us—not only without our help, but in spite of our sin and rebellion against Him. Paul said it well: "For while we were still helpless, at the right time Christ died for the ungodly" (Romans 5:6).

Let's define our term, and then we can move on. The simplest definition of grace is this: It is all that God is free to do for us based on the work of Christ. Underline the word *free,* because the thing that makes grace so incredible is that we couldn't possibly earn it, we will never be able to repay it, and we definitely don't deserve it. It's not that grace isn't costly. It's just that it isn't costly to us.

Another aspect of grace is that the supply of God's goodness is inexhaustible. That is, we will never reach the point in our lives where God's grace ceases to flow. It takes grace to get us saved, and it takes an inexhaustible supply to get us to heaven. We need God's grace as much today as we did the day we were saved. John Newton captured the immensity of grace when he wrote "'Tis grace hath brought me safe thus far, and grace will lead me home."

We're going to look at several of the Bible's great passages on grace, and before we are done I hope you will agree that we've saved the best for last. The church has a great message and ministry to deliver. I'm a "grace man" all the way. I preach about grace, think about it, dwell on it, rejoice in it, and revel in what God did for us because He is the God of grace.

THE EMBODIMENT OF GRACE

One of the Bible's greatest statements to churches and pastors on grace is found in Titus 2:11. Paul told Pastor Titus to teach the churches under his charge this truth: "For the grace of God has appeared, bringing salvation to all men." What does Paul mean by the appearing of God's grace? The apostle answered that in another place when he spoke of the grace that was granted to us "from all eternity, but now has been revealed by the appearing of our Savior Christ Jesus" (2 Timothy 1:9–10).

You see, God's grace has existed from all eternity. Some liberal theologians used to talk about the contrast between the God of wrath, vengeance, and judgment in the Old Testament and the God of love, grace, and forgiveness in the New Testament. No, God has always been a God of grace. The Old Testament is filled with stories of His gracious dealings with mankind. But before Christ appeared and sin was fully dealt with, we could say that God's grace was in the shadows. Like the sun on a cloudy day, God's grace was fully present before Christ, but it was not fully visible to us.

But when Christ came, it was like the clouds parting to reveal the sun shining in all of its glory. The grace of God appeared when Jesus came to earth. Jesus is the full-orbed expression of God's grace. John said of Jesus, "There was the true Light which, coming into the world, enlightens every man" (John 1:9). Jesus brought the saving purposes of God out of the shadows.

John then continued: "The Word became flesh, and dwelt among us, and we saw His glory, glory as of the only begotten of the Father, full of *grace* and truth" (v. 14, italics added). And finally: "For of His fullness we have all received, and *grace upon grace*. For the Law was given through Moses; *grace* and truth were realized through Jesus Christ" (vv. 16–17, italics added).

Grace is embodied in the Person of Christ. And the grace He brought at the cross brings salvation "to all men." I need to explain this phrase, because it does not mean that everyone is going to heaven. The idea is that through His death on the cross Christ paid for all sin, including the universal condemnation of all men inherited from Adam, what theologians call original sin. That means no person will go to hell for what Adam did in the Garden of Eden. Adam's corruption of the human race has been fully addressed in Christ. His death rendered all people "savable," so that anyone who goes to hell will go because of his or her own sin and refusal to accept Christ. Some people do not benefit from Christ's payment because they refuse His offer of salvation, but that doesn't diminish the sufficiency of His work.

But for those of us who have accepted the grace of God in the Person of Jesus Christ, God has opened a spiritual vault making available to us all of the resources needed to fulfill His purposes for our lives. All of it comes through the grace that appeared when Jesus came.

Now if grace did all of that for me, I want to learn everything about grace that I could possibly learn. I don't know about you, but I would not want to have to relate to God on the basis of the Law. The Law came through Moses and instructed God's people about His demands. But the Law provided no power to keep it, and it pre-scribed severe penalties for anyone who broke it. So we were doomed by the Law because while it is holy, we are completely unholy. Paul said, "We know that the Law is spiritual, but I am of flesh, sold into bondage to sin" (Romans 7:14).

The Law has only one standard: Obey and you will live, dis-obey and you will die. But the Bible says that when Christ came, the Law was set aside. "Christ is the end of the law for righteous-ness to everyone who believes" (Romans 10:4). Now that the Law of Moses has been taken out of the way, we have an unbroken link back to the Abrahamic covenant, which is based on promise and not law. We should get on our knees and faces every day to thank God that His grace was fully and finally revealed in Jesus Christ.

THE TEACHING OF GRACE

The job of the local church is to teach its members the awe-some truth of grace and help enable them to experience its reality and power in their lives. That's a big job, because the grace of God that has appeared in Christ has a lot to teach us. According to Titus 2:12, this grace "instruct[s] us to deny ungodliness and worldly desires and to live sensibly, righteously and godly in the present age." Grace not only redeems us, it reforms us. Living by grace opens up to us a whole new series of data that we were unaware of before. That's why we need to be instructed in the grace of God. It's an entirely new way of thinking and living. Churches that are not grace-oriented defeat, rather than develop, their members.

One reason I know that many churches need to be taught about grace is that so many Christians still try to relate to God based on law, as we said earlier. Another reason grace needs to teach us is that we are quick to forget that God's grace is free. One way you can test any preacher or any movement in the church is whether he or it wants you to pay for your manifestation of grace.

By that I mean if you have to send a gift to get a bottle of water from the Jordan River so you can experience God's blessing, something is wrong. If you have to send for an anointed handkerchief if you want to see God work in your life, that's not of God because He relates to you in grace, and His grace is free. The Bible says, "He who did not spare His own Son, but delivered Him over for us all, how will He not also with Him freely give us all things?" (Romans 8:32). God freely gave us Christ, which was the most expensive grace gift ever given. If God did not charge us for that, He is not about to start charging us now.

Grace also has a lot to teach us because some people in the church will take God's free grace to its illogical conclusion and say, "Since we are under grace and nothing can change that, let's live it up. Let's sin to our hearts' content because we're already forgiven."

That argument ought to sound familiar, for it's as old as the church. Paul addressed this issue in a classic passage that begins with these questions: "What shall we say then? Are we to continue in sin so that grace may increase?" (Romans 6:1). Then he gave the ringing answer: "May it never be! How shall we who died to sin still live in it?" (v. 2). Anyone who thinks grace is a license to sin doesn't understand the first thing about it.

We also have a strong answer to the "let us sin more" argument back in Titus 2:12. Grace teaches us to say no to ungodliness and yes to righteousness. Grace should motivate us to serve, not to sin. In fact, our service and dedication to God as people of grace ought to far outshine anything that was done under the Law. We serve in response to God's outpouring of favor upon us.

No one can buy grace. It's free, but when it gets hold of you, and when you really grasp the extent of what God did for you in Christ, no act of love or sacrifice God asks of you is too great.

There is so much more that grace has to teach us than we can cover in one chapter, or even in one book. Now if grace holds so much for us, it makes sense that this is the primary message Christians should be learning in their local churches. But it's amazing how many believers are still in kindergarten when it comes to understanding grace. Unfortunately, this is too often the case because the pastors themselves do not yet clearly understand the truth of grace.

I owned my car for about two years before I finally got around to reading the manual and finding out what that thing could do. It was embarrassing to discover all the things my car could do that I was ignorant of. For instance, I was still jumping out of the car and running around to unlock the trunk when there was a button at my fingertips to open the trunk.

Even worse, I was still messing with maps while trying to drive, making wrong turns and having to stop and ask for directions, when the car had a navigational system that would tell me every turn to make if I would just enter my destination. I found out the system would even redirect me if I missed a turn. This car was fully loaded, but it didn't do me much good because I didn't bother to read the manual. I needed instruction because I had never driven a car like that before. God has given us a fully loaded salvation by grace. But we need to be instructed in grace because we have never driven a car like this before.

Here's one more reason that churches must be grace oriented and teach their members how to live the Christian life from this orientation. Grace is different from law not only because the basis of acceptance is different. Grace is also different because it has built into it the power to enable you to fulfill God's perfect, righteous standards as embodied in the Law. In other words, grace enables what it expects.

That's important because God's expectations have never changed. God has always required that people say no to sin and yes to righteousness. But as we said above, the Law of Moses had no inherent power to enable our obedience. But, in grace, God writes His law on our hearts by the Holy Spirit and gives us the Spirit to indwell and empower us. The church should be a powerhouse of obedient Christians who know how to tap into the Spirit's enabling grace to live for Christ. The world should be looking at us and saying, "If that's what living by grace can do, I want in on it!"

You see, the world is used to living by rules. But rules alone don't change the human heart. If your heart is diseased and beyond repair, no number of rules about eating right and not smoking will fix it.

But if you receive a new heart through a transplant, nobody should have to lecture you about how to keep that heart working like new. You will respond in gratitude for your heart, which was a gift of grace that someone else provided.

Responding in obedience out of a relationship will always accomplish more than guilt-laced lectures rooted in rules alone. Most Christians aren't experiencing this truth because the churches they attend don't teach it.

THE FOCUS OF GRACE

Once we experience the grace of God in Christ, everything changes, including our focus. If you are looking for grace, you won't find it by looking in the mirror or anywhere else except to Jesus. The writer of Hebrews called us to "[fix] our eyes on Jesus, the author and perfecter of faith" (Hebrews 12:2).

Paul had the same idea in Titus 2:13, which continues the great sentence he began in verse 11: "Looking for the blessed hope and the appearing of the glory of our great God and Savior, Christ Jesus." Jesus is the focus of grace; our eyes need to be firmly fixed on Him.

You may say, "But this verse tells us to be looking for Christ's return. What does this future hope have to do with our living by grace today?" Oh, that's the best part. It has everything to do with today because Christ wants His church to keep Him first in its focus. Jesus' parable of the talents teaches us to conduct our lives as if the Master of the house could return at any moment (see Matthew 25:14–30).

In other words, looking for Christ's return in glory does not mean that we sit around doing nothing because He might come back today, or live any old way we please because He might not come back for a long time. When we live with our eyes on Jesus, looking for the blessed hope of His return, we will start to become more like Him. John said this about people who hope to see Jesus someday: "Everyone who has this hope fixed on Him purifies himself, just as He is pure" (1 John 3:3).

In Titus 2:11, Paul said that God's grace appeared in Christ at His first coming as Savior. Now we look for the second appearance of Christ, who will bring grace to fulfillment when He gathers the church to Himself and we celebrate the marriage supper of the Lamb (see Revelation 19:1–9).

Besides the fact that Jesus is our glorious God and Savior, there is another reason for us to keep our focus on Him. Jesus is also the perfect Man who knows exactly where you are and where you are coming from because He has been there. There is no tight spot you will ever be in, and no temptation you will ever face, that Jesus did not face Himself (see Hebrews 4:14–16).

You say, "Yes, but that was Jesus. He's the perfect Son of God. I don't have His ability to be victorious over sin."

Yes, you do. Jesus is ministering in heaven today as your Great High Priest to enable you to be an overcomer. Listen to this incredible invitation: "Therefore let us draw near with confidence to the throne of grace, so that we may receive mercy and find grace to help in time of need" (Hebrews 4:16).

The reason more believers aren't living in the victory that is ours by grace is that we are looking through the wrong end of the binoculars, so to speak. If you have ever tried that, you know how impossible it is to see what you want to see. We look at ourselves and see how weak and small we are, instead of looking at Christ and how mighty and all-glorious He is.

Now if you're wondering how you can get Christ in focus, the answer is found in your worship. I'm not just talking about what you do on Sunday morning, although that's important. I'm talking about a lifestyle of worship in which you learn the secret that the psalmist knew: "I will bless the Lord at all times; His praise shall continually be in my mouth. My soul will make its boast in the Lord; the humble will hear it and rejoice" (Psalm 34:1–2). You look to Christ by faith in your praise. You look to Him by faith in giving Him the glory that He deserves.

And when you do that, something important comes into focus. I love the next verse of Psalm 34: "O magnify the Lord with me, and let us exalt His name together" (v. 3). You may remember that we talked earlier about the way a magnifying glass makes an object look bigger to you. Let me remind you again that you can't make God any bigger than He is. He already inhabits and rules the universe. But you can make Him look bigger to you when you praise and worship Him.

Local churches, then, should not only bring their members out of their homes to worship, but also send them back home as worshipers who have a passionate desire to live under the umbrella of God's grace.

THE PEOPLE OF GRACE

There is one more verse I want us to consider in Titus 2. It's a great passage, because it tells the church who we are by God's grace. Speaking of Jesus Christ, Paul continued, "Who gave Himself for us to redeem us from every lawless deed, and to purify for Himself a people for His own possession, zealous for good deeds" (v. 14). God's grace has taken a bunch of rebels against Him and turned us into His family.

The reason you and I are going to make it is that we are special to God. My office at church receives as many as one hundred telephone calls a day. But I have another line that only my family has access to so that no matter what I am doing, family members can always get through if they need me because they are special. God says we are family now, with full access to His grace. And even when we fall, grace is there to catch us. The church is meant to be God's exhibit to a watching world of what His grace can do.

A man who had accepted Christ was trying to explain to his friends why his life was so different. Finally he reached down and picked up a worm, set it in the middle of a leaf, and then set the leaf on fire. The leaf began to curl up in the flame and close in on the worm. But just as the worm was about to be consumed by the fire, the man reached out and rescued the worm. "I'm the worm," he said to his friends. That's grace.

When God pulls you from the fire by His grace, there is nothing He cannot do through you. The church's motto ought to be, "I can do all things through Him who strengthens me" (Philippians 4:13). My own life and family are a testimony to the working of that grace.

I was born in the inner city of Baltimore. Today my neighborhood would be called the ghetto. Except for the house my parents still live in and a couple of others, the houses on my old block are boarded up. When we go back to visit my folks, we can see drug deals going down right there on the corner.

I grew up in a tough place, but God's grace in the Person of Jesus Christ reached down to my father and saved him when I was eleven years old. My daddy brought grace home, and I was saved. I had to go to special speech classes to learn to deal with the speech problem I told you about earlier. But God took a poor, inner-city boy and brought him through as the first member of his family to graduate from high school and the first one to go to college. Then God's grace carried me through a doctoral degree from seminary, and from a church with ten people in a house to the ministry he has blessed us with today. It's all because the grace of God appeared to the Evans family.

So when it comes to giving to God, I don't have to be pumped and primed. When it comes to serving God, I don't have to be begged. I know where I was, and I know where I would have been if grace had not appeared to me. I'm a grace man all the way because I have seen what it can do. The local church is designed to be a body of people who have discovered grace and can say with the spiritual, "Free at last, free at last. Thank God Almighty, we're free at last."

THE FREEDOM OF GRACE

Freedom is wonderful, especially when Jesus Christ sets you truly free. His own declaration is, "If the Son makes you free, you will be free indeed" (John 8:36). The final blessing of grace that churches should orient their members to is the freedom that grace brings.

The history of Texas is marked by the tragedy of slaves who were still in bondage two years after Abraham Lincoln signed the Emancipation Proclamation because the word of their freedom took that long to reach them. Equally tragic is the case of slaves who refused their liberation and wanted to stay on the plantation because slavery was all they had ever known. It doesn't take chains and overseers to keep people in slavery if they willingly submit to their bondage. The reason so many Christians are still in bondage to sin, self, and circumstances is that so many churches are not delivering the message of the freedom God's people have attained through grace.

If there is anything still holding you in bondage, the message of grace is a message of freedom for you. It's found in Galatians 5:1: "It was for freedom that Christ set us free; therefore keep standing firm and do not be subject again to a yoke of slavery." If you have been set free from sin and death by Jesus Christ, stand firm in your freedom and don't let the devil put his yoke around your neck again. That was Paul's message to the church in Galatia, and it's a message that churches desperately need to understand and preach today.

The Burden of the Law

A lot of people misunderstand the nature of true freedom. To many people, freedom means they have the right to do anything they want. But biblical freedom is liberty from the bondage of sin to enjoy a new relationship with Christ and do what is right. Freedom doesn't mean the absence of boundaries, but the ability to use your full potential within the boundaries God has set.

Imagine a running back who takes the handoff from the quarterback and takes off up field. As he is running he says, "I want to be free. I don't want to be hemmed in by these sidelines." So he runs off the field and into the stands, heads out to the parking lot and runs around to the other end of the stadium, then veers back into the stadium, down an aisle, onto the field, and into his opponent's end zone. He may start doing his touchdown dance, but his effort won't count because he didn't stay within the rules of the game. He did not fulfill his purpose as a member of his team.

Biblical freedom is the ability and the privilege God gives you to fulfill your divinely ordained purpose. Jesus called it having life "abundantly" (John 10:10). Paul raised the issue of freedom in Galatians 5 because he was being pursued and harassed by a group of people called Judaizers, or legalists, who wanted to hold Gentile believers hostage to the Mosaic Law. These people had come to the local churches of Galatia and were tying the believers there in knots with their teaching.

Church-based and church-sanctioned legalism is a lethal approach to the Christian life. It is a self-sufficient way of living because it all depends on you following the rules and checking off your obedience. The legalism that the Judaizers wanted to impose on Gentile Christians involved submitting to circumcision as a sign that the person was coming under obligation to the Law. So Paul continued: "Behold I, Paul, say to you that if you receive circumcision, Christ will be of no benefit to you" (Galatians 5:2).

God certainly has standards, as we have said. But the provision God has made for believers to keep them is not by straining to follow a legalistic list of rules, but by responding to a relationship based on grace. Jesus said, "My yoke is easy and My burden is light" (Matthew 11:30). John wrote, "For this is the love of God, that we keep His commandments; and His commandments are not burdensome" (1 John 5:3).

When grace is our motivation, there is joy in keeping God's commands. But the Galatians were being burdened and troubled (see Galatians 5:12) by the Judaizers' attempts to bring them under the Law's yoke. Law-keeping frustrates God's people and robs them of their freedom and joy and purpose. Paul had made a profound statement about the Law earlier in Galatians: "If a law had been given which was able to impart life, then righteousness would indeed have been based on law" (3:21). The issue of whether any person can be made right before God by the Law was settled a long time ago, and the verdict was no, not one.

Freedom from the Law

So how do we experience the freedom Christ purchased for us on the cross? We need to get rid of that plantation mentality. Don't let anyone put a yoke of religious legalism on your neck. Paul was so worked up about this that he warned the Galatians: "I testify again to every man who receives circumcision, that he is under obligation to keep the whole Law. You have been severed from Christ, you who are seeking to be justified by law; *you have fallen from grace*" (5:3–4, italics added).

Paul's point is tragically clear. Churches can actually disconnect their members from Christ instead of connecting them with Him by teaching a law orientation rather than a grace orientation.

This is serious stuff. You can't pick and choose which laws you want to obey. You need to understand that legalism is a package deal, all or nothing. What's more, the Bible says, law and grace are mutually exclusive. "If it is by grace, it is no longer on the basis of works" (Romans 11:6). Trying to live by the Law severs you from Christ, which is like cutting off the power cord to an appliance. Nothing happens when you try to use it because there is no power transfer. This helps explain the powerlessness in so many churches in spite of the fact that they regularly teach the Bible.

Many people think that the phrase "fallen from grace" means that you can lose your salvation. That's impossible for a true believer. You don't lose your salvation when you surrender grace for Law. But you lose something important because you are no longer operating under a grace standard. Law tells you what to do, gives you the penalty for failing, and then condemns you when you fail. Grace says God will set you free to keep His commands out of love for what He has already done for you. Which standard do you want to live by?

When I go to the cafeteria, I always drink sweetened tea. There are two ways to make iced tea sweet. You can either take unsweetened tea and stir in your own sugar, or you can order tea that was sweetened by the restaurant staff when it was made. The problem with doing it yourself is that you never get it all dissolved the right way, so there is always some sugar residue at the bottom of the glass to make the last few gulps too sweet.

But when the restaurant sweetens the tea, the sugar is dissolved just right because it is added when the tea is brewing and the water is still hot. That way the sugar becomes a component of the tea itself instead of a late add-on.

A lot of churches try to add to grace, mixing it up with Law and self-effort and hoping it will taste right. But when the Holy Ghost gets hold of you and the fire from heaven melts your heart, grace becomes a vital component of your walk with God and He creates a grace relationship out of which good works come. You are no longer working to make it right, but working because God made it right.

Paul told the Galatians not to abandon grace. There is no need to, because God's grace is inexhaustible. James says He gives "a greater grace" (James 4:6). Paul said that grace abounds to cover sin (see Romans 5:20). Remember when that police officer pulled you over for a violation? Your palms became sweaty as you handed the officer your license and waited for the ticket that you knew was coming because you knew you were guilty. But when the officer said, "Just be careful" and let you go free with a warning, there was a sense of relief because you had just experienced grace. At that moment you were probably more than ready to give testimony to the joy and freedom that grace brings.

My granddaughter's name is Kariss, which is the Greek word for grace. So whenever I call Kariss, I am literally saying, "Come here, grace." She usually spends the night with me on Wednesday nights, and she hears her name called about one hundred times because she usually gets what she wants from Poppy. And when I call, Kariss responds, because she knows the result of my calling her is usually more grace. Kariss is spoiled, but it's all right because I am the grandfather. It's legal for grandparents to spoil their grandchildren.

There's something about hearing your name called when your name is grace, and the result of having your name called is more grace. God says we are His grace children, and we know that when

He calls our name it's because He loves us and wants to be with us and wants to give us the best He has. And when we hear God calling us, we want to answer because grace makes us want to respond. May God help your church ever to teach and preach, and never to surrender, grace!

CONCLUSION

I used to be the chaplain for the Dallas Cowboys football team. As chaplain I led a weekly Bible study with the team and provided personal counseling for the players. I also used to go to the practice field and work out with the team, and in so doing I came to learn many of the team's plays.

One play called for the quarterback to throw a long pass to the wide receiver for a touchdown, with the halfback peeling off to the side in case the opposing team blitzed the quarterback before he had time to throw the long pass. If the blitz came, the halfback would become the alternate receiver in place of the original plan that called for the long pass to the wide receiver.

God's original plan was to throw a long pass to Israel, who was to receive the gospel ball and bring in the kingdom. However, Satan blitzed the play, seeking to stop the program of God. But God had another receiver going out on the other side called the church.

The church is God's alternative in history. Although it was always in God's plan, the church is a mystery that was not revealed to the earlier generations of His people. It was uniquely created to be God's institution for developing Christians and impacting the world. As goes the church, so go the spiritual lives of its members, and so goes the culture. The church in its various local expressions around the world is designed to score touchdowns for the kingdom of God.

INDEX OF SCRIPTURE

INDEX OF SUBJECTS

The Understanding God Series

Totally Saved

*Understanding, Experiencing and
Enjoying the Greatness of Your Salvation*

In *Totally Saved* Tony Evans explores justification, propitiation, redemption, reconciliation, forgiveness, and other biblical truths as he considers what it means to be totally saved.

ISBN: 0-8024-6824-1

Our God Is Awesome

Encountering the Greatness of Our God

Tony Evans has done a masterful job of unfolding the rich truth about God and who He is. He writes with uncommon clarity, accuracy and warmth. This book will be a treasured resource for all who desire to know God better.

– John MacArthur, Pastor, Grace Community Church of the Valley.

ISBN: 0-8024-4850-X

Returning To Your First Love

Putting God Back In First Place

Tony Evans has done to us all a service in focusing the biblical spotlight on the absolute necessity of keeping our love of Christ as the central passion of our hearts. Any earnest Christian knows how easy it is to become so absorbed in doing things for Christ that we forget to cultivate our love relationship with Him.

– Charles Stanley, Pastor, First Baptist Church in Atlanta, Author

ISBN: 0-8024-4851-8

The Promise

Experiencing God's Greatest Gift the Holy Spirit

Here is a book that points us to the Spirit's way to purity and power. Every chapter is appropriately titled "Experiencing the Spirit's. . . ." May this work help all who read it to do so.

– Dr. Charles Ryrie, Professor, Dallas Theological Seminary

ISBN: 0-8024-4852-6

Who Is This King of Glory?

Experiencing the Fullness of Christ's Work in Our Lives

In this practical, biblically-based volume, Tony Evans examines Jesus, "the greatest of all subjects," from three different perspectives:

- His uniqueness
- His authority
- Our appropriate response to Him

ISBN: 0-8024-4854-2

The Battle Is the Lord's

Waging Victorious Spiritual Warfare

We're in a war, but Christ has given us the victory. In *The Battle is the Lord's*, Tony Evans reveals Satan's strategies, teaches how you can fight back against the forces of darkness, and shows you how to find deliverance from the devil's snares.

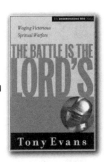

ISBN: 0-8024-4855-0

The Best Is Yet to Come

Bible Prophecies Through the Ages

Tony Evans propels you past the hype and confusion of prophecy, straight to the Source. He skillfully unlocks the secrets of the prophetic program, simultaneously unveiling the future for all to read and understand.

ISBN: 0-8024-4856-9

What Matters Most

Four Absolute Necessities in Following Christ

God's goal for believers is that they become more like Christ. But what does that mean? In *What Matters Most*, Tony Evans explores the four essential elements of discipleship:

- Worship
- Fellowship
- Education
- Outreach

MOODY
PUBLISHERS
THE NAME YOU CAN TRUST®

ISBN: 0-8024-4853-4

www.MoodyPublishers.com

MOODY
PUBLISHERS

THE NAME YOU CAN TRUST®

GOD'S GLORIOUS CHURCH TEAM

ACQUIRING EDITOR
Greg Thornton

DEVELOPMENT EDITOR
Phil Rawley

COPY EDITOR
Cheryl Dunlop

BACK COVER COPY
Smartt Guys

COVER DESIGN
Smartt Guys

COVER PHOTO
Donald Fuller

INTERIOR DESIGN
Ragont Design

PRINTING AND BINDING
Versa Press, Inc.

The typeface for the text of this book is
Berkeley